THE NIHONGI

CONTENTS

THE AGE OF THE GODS 9

THE LAWS OF ROTOKU TENNO 37

THE LATER RULERS 75

THE AGE OF THE GODS

BOOK I

Of old, Heaven and Earth were not yet separated, and the In and Yo not yet divided. They formed a chaotic mass like an egg which was of obscurely defined limits and contained germs.

The purer and clearer part was thinly drawn out, and formed Heaven, while the heavier and grosser element settled down and became Earth.

The finer element easily became a united body, but the consolidation of the heavy and gross element was accomplished with difficulty.

Heaven was therefore formed first, and Earth was established subsequently.

Thereafter divine beings were produced between them.

Hence it is said that when the world began to be created, the soil of which lands were composed floated about in a manner which might be compared to the floating of a fish sporting on the surface of the water.

At this time a certain thing was produced between Heaven and Earth. It was in form like a reed-shoot. Now this became transformed into a God, and was called Kuni-toko-tachi no Mikoto.

Next there was Kuni no sa-tsuchi no Mikoto, and next Toyo-kumu-nu no Mikoto, in all three deities

These were pure males spontaneously developed by the operation of the principle of Heaven.

In one writing it is said: "'When Heaven and Earth began, a thing existed in the midst of the Void. Its shape may not be described. Within it a deity was spontaneously produced, whose name was Kuni-toko-tachi no Mikoto, also called Kuni-soko-tachi no Mikoto. Next there was Kuni no sa-tsuchi no Mikoto, also called Kuni no sa-tachi no Mikoto. Next there was Toyo-kuni-nushi no Mikoto, also called Toyo-kumu-nu no Mikoto, Toyo-ka-fushi-no no Mikoto, Uki-fu-no-toyo-kahi no Mikoto, Toyo-kuni-no no Mikoto, Toyo-kuhi-no no Mikoto, Ha-ko-kuni-no no Mikoto, or Mi-no no Mikoto."

In one writing it is said: "Of old, when the land was Young and the earth young, it floated about, as it were floating oil. At this time a thing was produced within the land, in shape like a reed-shoot when it sprouts forth. From this there was a deity developed, whose name was Umashi-ashi-kabi-hiko-ji no Mikoto. Next there was Kuni no toko-tachi no Mikoto, and next Kuni no sa-tsuchi no Mikoto."

In one writing it is said: "When Heaven and Earth were in a state of chaos, there was first of all a deity, whose name was Umashi-ashi-kabi-hiko-ji no Mikoto. Next there was Kuni-soko-tachi no Mikoto."

In one writing it is said: "When Heaven and Earth began, there were deities produced together, whose names were, first, Kuni-no-toko-tachi no Mikoto, and next Kuni no satsuchi no Mikoto." It is further stated: "The names of the gods which were produced in the Plain of High Heaven were Ama no mi-naka-nushi no Mikoto, next Taka-mi-musubi no Mikoto, next Kami-mi-musubi no Mikoto."

In one writing it is said: "Before Heaven and Earth were produced, there was something which might be compared to a cloud floating over the sea. It had no place of attachment for its root. In the midst of this a thing was generated which resembled a reed-shoot when it is first produced in the mud. This became straightway transformed into human shape and was called Kuni no toko-tachi no Mikoto."

[In this fashion the "Nihongi "rambles on, telling much the same legends as the "Kojiki", until it comes to the days of the immediate ancestors of Jimmu Tenno. There were then two brothers, grandchildren of the goddess Ama-terasu.]

The elder brother Ho-no-susori no Mikoto had by nature a sea-gift; the younger brother Hiko-ho-ho-demi no Mikoto had by nature a mountain-gift. In the beginning the two brothers, the elder and the younger, conversed together, saying: "Let us for a trial exchange gifts." They eventually exchanged them, but neither of them gained aught by doing so. The elder brother repented his bargain, and returned to the younger brother his bow and arrows, asking for his fish-hook to be given back to him. But the younger brother had already lost the elder brother's fish-book, and there was no means of finding it. He accordingly made another new hook which he offered to his elder brother. But his elder brother refused to accept it, and demanded the old hook. The younger brother, grieved at this, forthwith took his cross-sword and forged from it new fish-hooks, which he heaped up in a winnowing tray, and offered to his brother. But his elder brother was wroth, and said: "These are not my old fish-hook: though they are many, I will not take them." And be continued repeatedly to demand it vehemently. Therefore Hiko-hoho-demi no Mikoto's grief was exceedingly profound, and be went and made moan by the shore of the sea. There he met Shiho-tsutsu no Oji. The old man inquired of him saying - "Why dost thou grieve here?" He answered and told him the matter from first to last. The old man said: "Grieve no more. I will arrange this matter for thee." So he made a basket without interstices, and placing in it Hoho-demi no Mikoto, sank it in the sea. Forthwith he found himself at a pleasant strand, where he abandoned the basket, and proceeding on his way, suddenly arrived at the palace of the Sea-god. This palace was provided with battlements and turrets, and had stately towers. Before the gate there was a well, and over the well there grew a many branched cassia-tree, with wide-spreading boughs and leaves. Now Hiko-hoho-demi no Mikoto went up to the foot of this tree and loitered about. After some time a beautiful woman appeared, and, pushing open the door, came forth. She at length took a jewel-vessel and approached. She was about to draw water, when, raising her eyes, she saw him, and was alarmed. Returning within, she spoke to her father and mother, saying: "There is a rare stranger at the foot of the tree before the gate." The god of the Sea thereupon prepared an eightfold cushion and led him in. When they bad taken their seats, he inquired of him the object of his coming. Then Hiko-hoho-demi no Mikoto explained to him, in reply, all the circumstances. The Sea-god accordingly assembled the fishes, both great and small, and required of them an answer. They all said: "We know not. Only the Red-woman has had a sore mouth for some time past and has not come." She was therefore peremptorily summoned to appear and on her mouth being examined the lost hook was actually found.

After this, Hiko-hoho-demi no Mikoto took to wife the Seagod's daughter, Toyo-tama-hime, and dwelt in the sea-palace. For three years he enjoyed peace and pleasure, but still had a longing for his own country, and therefore sighed deeply from time to time. Toyo-tama-hime heard this and told her father, saying: "The Heavenly Grandchild often sighs as if in grief. It may be that it is the sorrow of long in, for his country. "The god of the Sea thereupon drew to him Hiko-hoho-demi no Mikoto, and addressing him in an easy, familiar way, said: "If the Heavenly Grandchild desires to return to his country I will send him back." So he gave him the fish-hook which he had found, and in doing so instructed him, saying: "When thou givest this fish-hook to thy elder brother, before giving it to him call to it secretly, and say, 'A poor hook.'" He further presented to him the jewel of the flowing tide and the jewel of the ebbing tide, and instructed him, saying: "If thou dost dip the tide-flowing jewel, the tide will suddenly flow, and therewithal thou shalt drown thine elder brother. But in case thy elder brother should repent and beg forgiveness, if, on the contrary, thou dip the tide-ebbing jewel, the tide will spontaneously ebb, and therewithal thou shalt save him. If thou harass him in this way, thy elder brother will of his own accord render submission.

When the Heavenly Grandchild was about to set out on his return journey, Toyo-tama-hime addressed him, saying: "Thy handmaiden is already pregnant, and the time of her delivery is not far off. On a day when the winds and waves are raging, I will surely come forth to the sea-shore, and I pray thee that thou wilt make for me a parturition-house, and await me there."

When Hiko-hoho-demi no Mikoto returned to his palace, he complied implicitly with the instructions of the Sea-god, and the elder brother, Ho-no-susori no Mikoto, finding himself in the utmost straits, of his own accord admitted his offense, and said: "Henceforward I will be thy subject to perform mimic dances for thee. I beseech thee mercifully to spare my life." Thereupon he at length yielded his petition, and spared him. This Ho-no-susori no Mikoto was the first ancestor of the Kimi of Wobashi in Ata.

After this Toyo-tama-hime fulfilled her promise, and, bringing with her her younger sister, Tama-yori-hime, bravely confronted the winds and waves, and came to the sea-shore. When the time of her delivery was at hand, she besought Hiko-hoho-demi no Mikoto, saying: "When thy handmaiden is in travail, I pray thee do not look upon her." However, the Heavenly Grandchild could not restrain himself, but went secretly and peeped in. Now Toyo-tama-hime was just in childbirth, and had changed into a dragon. She was greatly ashamed, and said: "Hadst thou not disgraced me, I would have made the sea and land communicate with each other, and forever prevented them from being sundered. But now that thou hast disgraced me, wherewithal shall friendly feelings be knit together?" So she wrapped the infant inrushes, and abandoned it on the sea-shore. Then she barred the sea-path, and passed away. Accordingly the child was called Hiko-nagisa-take-u-gaya-fuki-ahezu no Mikoto.

Another account says that when the child was born, the Heavenly Grandchild approached and made inquiry, saying: "By what name ought the child to be called?" She answered and said: "Let him be called Hiko-nagisa-take-u-gayafuki-ahezu no Mikoto." Having said so, she took her departure straight across the sea. Then Hiko-hoho-demi no Mikoto made a song, saying:

> Whatever befalls me,
> Ne'er shall I forget my love
> With whom I slept
> In the islands of wild-ducks—
> The birds of the offing."

After this, when Toyo-tama-hime heard what a fine boy her child was, her heart was greatly moved with affection' and she wished to come back and bring him up herself. But she could not rightly do so, and therefore she sent her younger sister Tama-yori-hime to nurture him. Now when Toyotama-hime sent Tama-yori-hime, she offered (to Hoho-demi no Mikoto) the following verse in answer:

> Some may boast
> Of the splendor
> Of red jewels,
> But those worn by my lord—
> It is they which are admirable."

These two stanzas, one sent, and one in reply, are what are termed age-uta.

Another account says that when the Sea-god gave the fishhook to Hiko-hoho-demi no Mikoto, he instructed him, saying: "When thy elder brother's fish-hook is returned to him, let the Heavenly Grandchild say: 'Let it be to all thy descendants, of whatever degree of relationship, a poor hook, a paltry poor hook.' When thou hast thus spoken, spit thrice, and give it to him. Moreover, when thy elder brother goes to sea a-fishing, let the Heavenly Grandchild stand on the seashore and do that which raises the wind. Now that which raises the wind is whistling. If thou doest so,

I will forthwith stir up the wind of the offing and the wind of the shore, and will overwhelm and vex him with the scurrying waves." Ho no ori no Mikoto returned, and obeyed implicitly the instructions of the god. When a day came on which the elder brother went a-fishing, the younger brother stood on the shore of the sea, and whistled. Then there arose a sudden tempest, and the elder brother was forthwith overwhelmed and harassed. Seeing no means of saving his life, lie besought his younger brother from afar, saying: "Thou hast dwelt long in the ocean-plain, and must possess some excellent art. I pray thee teach it to me. If thou save my life, my descendants of all degrees of relationship shall not leave the neighborhood of thy precinct, but shall act as thy mime-vassals." Thereupon the younger brother left off whistling, and the wind again returned to rest. So the elder brother recognized the younger brother's power, and freely admitted his fault. But the younger brother was wroth, and -would hold no converse with him. Hereupon the elder brother, with nothing but his waistcloth on, and smearing the palms of his bands and his face with red earth, said to his younger brother: "Thus do I defile my body, and make my self thy mime forever." So kicking up his feet, he danced along and practiced the manner of his drowning struggles. First of all, when the tide reached his feet, he did the foot divination ; when it reached his knees, he raised up his feet; when it reached his thighs, he ran round in a circle; when it reached his loins, he rubbed his loins; when it reached his sides, he placed his hands upon his breast; when it reached his neck, be threw up his hands, waving his palms. From that time until now, this custom has never ceased.

Now, when the child Hiko-nagisa-take-u-gaya-fuki-abezu no Mikoto grew up, he took his aunt Tama-yori-hime as his consort, and had by her in all four male children. Long after, .Hiko-nagisa-take-u-gaya-fuki-ahezu no Mikoto died, in the palace of the western country, and was buried in the Misasagi on the top of Mount Ahira in Hiuga.

BOOK III

THE EMPEROR KAMI-YAMATO IHARE-BIKO

The Emperor Kami Yamato Ihare-biko's personal name was Hiko-hoho-demi. [This is the legendary conquerer known to later ages as Jimmu Tenno.] He was the fourth child of Hiko-nagisa-take-u-gaya-fuki-ahezu no Mikoto. His mother's name was Tama-yori-hime, daughter of the Sea-god. From his birth, this Emperor was of clear intelligence and resolute will. At the age of fifteen he was made heir to the throne. When be grew up, he married Ahira-tsu-hime, of the district of Ata in the province of Hiuga, and made her his consort. By her he had Tagishi-mimi no Mikoto and Kisu-mimi no Mikoto.

When he reached the age of forty-five, he addressed his elder brothers and his children, saying: "Of old, our Heavenly deities Taka-mi-musubi no Mikoto, and Oho-hiru-me no Mikoto, pointing to this land of fair rice-ears of the fertile reed-plain, gave it to our Heavenly ancestor, Hiko-ho no ninigi no Mikoto. Thereupon Hiko-ho no ninigi no Mikoto, throwing open the barrier of Heaven and clearing a cloud-path, urged on his superhuman course until he came to rest. At this time the world was given over to widespread desolation. It was an age of darkness and disorder. In this gloom, therefore, be fostered justice, arid so governed this western border. Our Imperial ancestors and Imperial parent, like gods, like sages, accumulated happiness and amassed glory. Many years elapsed. From the date when our Heavenly ancestor descended until now it is over 1,792,470 years .But the remote regions do not yet enjoy the blessings of Imperial rule. Every town has always been allowed to have its lord, and every village its chief, who, each one for himself, makes division of territory and practises mutual aggression and conflict.

"Now I have heard from the Ancient of the Sea, that in the East there is a fair land encircled on all sides by blue mountains. -Moreover, there is there one who flew down riding in a Heavenly Rock-boat. I think that this land will undoubtedly be suitable for the extension of the Heavenly task,' so that its,Iorv should fill the universe. It is, doubtless, the center of the world." The person who flew down was, I believe, Nigi-haya-hi. Why should we not proceed thither, and make it the capital?"

All the Imperial Princess answered, and said: "The truth of this is manifest. This thought is constantly present to our minds also. Let us go thither quickly." This was the year Kinoye Tora (51st) of the Great Year. (667 B.C.)

In that year, in winter, on the Kanoto Tori day (the 5th) of the 10th month, the new moon of which was on the day Hinoto Mi, the Emperor in person led the Imperial Princes and a naval force on an expedition against the East. When be arrived at the Haya-suhi gate, there was there a fisherman who came riding in a boat. The Emperor summoned him, and then inquired of him, saying: "Who art thou?" He answered and said: "Thy servant is a Country-god, and his name is Utsu-hiko. I angle for fish in the bays of ocean. Hearing that the son of the Heavenly deity was coming, therefore I forthwith came to receive him." Again he inquired of him, saying: "Canst thou act as my guide?" He answered and said: "I will do so." The Emperor ordered the end of a pole of shihi wood to be given to the fisher, and caused him to be taken and pulled into the Imperial vessel, of which be was made pilot. A name was specially granted him, and he was called Shibi-ne-tsu-hiko." He was the first ancestor of the Yamato no Atahe.

Proceeding on their voyage, they arrived at Usa in the land of Tsukushi. At this time there appeared the ancestors of the Kuni-tsu-ko of Usa, named Usa-tsu-hiko and Usatsu-hime. They built a palace raised on one pillar on the banks of the River Usa, and offered them a banquet. Then, by Imperial command, Usa-tsu-hime was given in marriage to the Emperor's attendant minister Ama no tane no Mikoto. Now Ama no tane no Mikoto was the remote ancestor of the Nakatomi Uji.

11th month, 9th day. The Emperor arrived at the harbor of Oka in the land of Tsukushi.

12th month, 27th day. He arrived at the province of A-ki, where he dwelt in the Palace of Ye.

(666 B.C.) The year Kinoto U, Spring, 3rd month, 6th day. Going onward, he entered the land of Kibi, and built a temporary palace, in which he dwelt. It was called the Palace of Takasbima. Three years passed, during which time be set in order the helms of his ships, and prepared a store of provisions. It was his desire by a single effort to subdue the Empire.

(663 B.C.) The year Tsuchinoye Muma, Spring, 2nd month, 11th day. The Imperial forces at length proceeded eastward, the prow of one ship touching the stern of another. Just when they reached Cape Naniha they encountered a current of great swiftness. Whereupon that place was called Nami-haya (wave-swift) or Nami-hana (wave-flower). It is now called Naniha which is a corruption of this.

3rd mouth, 10th day. Proceeding upward against the stream, they went straight on, and arrived at the port of Awokumo no Shira-date, in the township of Kusaka, in the province of Kafuebi.

Summer, 4th month, 9th day. The Imperial forces in martial array marched on to Tatsuta. The road was narrow and precipitous, and the men were unable to march abreast, so they returned and again endeavored to go eastward, crossing over Mount Ikoma. In this way they entered the inner country.

Now when Naga-sune-hiko heard this, be said: "The object of the children of the Heavenly deity in coming hither is assuredly to rob me of my country." so be straightway levied all the forces under his dominion, and intercepted them at the Hill of Kusaka. A battle was engaged, and Itsuse no Mikoto was hit by a random arrow on the elbow. The Imperial forces were unable to advance against the enemy. The Emperor was vexed, and revolved in his inmost heart a divine plan, saying: "I am the descendant of the Sun-goddess, and if I proceed against the Sun to attack the enemy, I shall act contrary to the way of Heaven. Better to retreat and make a show of weakness. Then sacrificing to the gods of Heaven and Earth, and bringing on our backs the might of the Sun-goddess, let us follow her rays and trample them down. If we do so, the enemy will assuredly be routed of themselves, and we shall not stain our swords with blood." They all said: "It is good." Thereupon he gave orders to the army, saying: "Wait a while, and advance no further." So he withdrew his forces, and the enemy also did not dare to attack him. He then retired to the port of Kusaka, where he set up shields, and made a warlike show. Therefore the name of this port was changed to Tatetsu which is now corrupted into Tadetsu.

Before this, at the battle of Kusaka, there was a man who hid in a great tree, and by so doing escaped danger. So pointing to this tree, he said. "I am grateful to it, as to my mother." Therefore the people of the day called that place Omo no ki no Mura .

5th month, 8th day. The army arrived at the port of Yamaki in Chinu (also called Port Yama no wi). Now Itsuse no Mikoto's arrow wound was extremely painful. He grasped his sword, and striking a martial attitude, said "How exasperating it is that a man should die of a wound received at the hands of slaves, and should not revenge it!" The people of that day therefore called the place Wo no minato.

Proceeding onward, they reached Mount Kama in the land of Kii, where Itsuse no Mikoto died in the army, and was therefore buried at Mount Kama.

6th month, 23rd day. The army arrived at the village of Nagusa, where they put to death the Tohe of Nagusa. Finally they crossed the moor of Sano, and arrived at the village of kami in Kuniano. Here be embarked in the rock-boat of Heaven, and leading his army, proceeded onward by slow degrees. In the midst of the sea, they suddenly met with a violent wind, and the Imperial vessel was tossed about. Then Ina-ihi no Mikoto exclaimed and said: "Alas! my ancestors were Heavenly deities, and my mother was a goddess of the Sea. Why do they harass me by land, and why, moreover, do they harass me by sea." When he had said this, he drew his sword and plunged into the sea, where he became changed into the god Sabi-mochi Mike Irino no Mikoto, also indignant at this, said: "My mother and my aunt are both Sea-goddesses: why do they raise great billows to overwhelm us? "So treading upon the waves, he went to the Eternal Land. The Emperor was now alone with the Imperial Prince Tagishi-mimi no Mikoto. Leading his army forward, he arrived at Port Arazaka in Kumano (also called Nishiki Bay), where he put to death the Tobe of Nishiki. At this time the gods belched up a poisonous vapor, from which every one suffered. For this reason the Imperial army was again unable to exert itself. Then there was there a man by name Kuniano no Takakuraji, who unexpectedly had a dream, in which Ama-terasu no Ohokami spoke to Take-mika-tsuchi no Kami, saying: "I still hear a sound of disturbance from the Central Land of Reed-Plains. Do thou again go and chastise it." Take-mika-tsuchi no Kami answered and said: "Even if I go not, I can send down my sword, with which I subdued the land, upon which the country will of its own accord become peaceful." To this Ama-terasu no Kami assented. Thereupon Take-mik-a-tsuchi no Kami addressed Takakuraji, saying: "My sword, which is called Futsu no Mitama, I will now place in thy storehouse. Do thou take it and present it to the Heavenly Grandchild." Takakuraji said "Yes," and thereupon awoke. The next morning, as instructed in his dream, be opened the storehouse, and on looking in, there was indeed there a sword which had fallen down (from Heaven), and was standing upside down on the plank floor of the storehouse. So he took it and offered it to the Emperor. At this time the Emperor happened to be asleep. He awoke suddenly, and said: "What a long time I have slept! "On inquiry he found that the troops who had been affected by the poison had all recovered their senses and were afoot. The Emperor then endeavored to advance into the interior, but among, the mountains it was so precipitous that there was no road by which they could travel, and they wandered about not knowing whither to direct their march. Then Amaterasu no Obo-kami instructed the Emperor in a dream of the night, saying: "I will now send thee the Yata-garasu," make it thy guide through the land." Then there did indeed appear the Yata-garasu flying down from the Void. The Emperor said: "The coming of this crow is in due accordance with my auspicious dream. How grand! How splendid! My Imperial ancestor, Ama-terasu no Oho-kami, desires therewith to assist me in creating the hereditary institution.'

At this time Hi no Omi no Mikoto, ancestor of the Ohotomo House, taking with him Oho-kume as commander of the main body, guided by the direction taken by the crow, looked up to it and followed after, until at length they arrived at the district of Lower Uda. Therefore they named the place which they reached the village of Ukechi in Uda.

At this time, by an Imperial order, he commended Hi no Omi no Mikoto, saying: "Thou art faithful and brave, and art, moreover, a successful guide. Therefore will I give thee a new name, and will call thee Michi no Omi."

Autumn, 8th month, 2nd day. The Emperor sent to summon Ukeshi the Elder and Ukeshi the Younger. These two were chiefs of the district of Uda. Now Ukesbi the Elder did not come. But Ukeshi the Younger came, and making obeisance at the gate of the camp, declared as follows: "Thy servant's elder brother, Ukeshi the Elder, shows signs of resistance. Hearing that the descendant of Heaven was about to arrive, he forthwith raised an army with which to make an attack. But having seen from afar the might of the Imperial army, be was afraid, and did not dare to oppose it. Therefore be has secretly placed his troops in ambush, and has built for the occasion a new palace, in the ball of which he has prepared engines. It is his intention to invite the Emperor to a banquet there, and then to do him a mischief.

I pray that his treachery be noted, and that good care be taken to make preparation against it." The Emperor straightway sent Michi no Omi no Mikoto to observe the signs of his opposition. Michi no Omi no Mikoto clearly ascertained his hostile intentions, and being greatly enraged, shouted at him in a blustering manner: "Wretch! thou shalt thyself dwell in the house which thou hast made." So grasping his sword, and drawing his bow, he urged him and drove him within it. Ukeshi the Elder being guilty before Heaven, and the matter not admitting of excuse, of his own accord trod upon the engine and was crushed to death. His body was then brought out and decapitated, and the blood which flowed from it reached above the ankle. Therefore that place was called Uda no Chi-hara. After this Ukeshi the Younger prepared a great feast of beef and sake with which he entertained the Imperial army. The Emperor distributed this flesh and sake to the common soldiers, upon which they sang the following verses:

> In the high castle/tree of Uda tree
> I set a snare for woodcock,
> And waited,
> But no woodcock came to it;
> A valiant whale came to it.

This is called a Kume song. At the present time, when the Department of Music performs this song, there is still the measurement of great and small by the hand, as well as a distinction of coarse and fine in the notes of the voice. This is by a rule handed down from antiquity.

After this the Emperor wished to inspect the land of Yoshino, so taking personal command of the light troops, he made a progress round by way of Ukechi mura in Uda.

When he came to Yoshino, there was a man who came out of a well. He shone, and had a tail. The Emperor inquired of him, saying: "What man art thou?" He answered and said: Thy servant is a local deity, and his name is Wi-hi-kari." He it is who was the first ancestor of the Yoshino no Obito. Proceeding a little farther, there was another man with a tail, who burst open a rock and came forth from it. The Emperor inquired of him, saying: "What man art thou?" He answered and said: "Thy servant is the child of Iha-oshi-wake." It is he who was the first ancestor of the Kuzu of Yoshino.

Then skirting the river, he proceeded westward, when there appeared another man, who had made a fish-trap and was catching fish. On the Emperor making inquiry of him, he answered and said: "Thy servant is the son of Nihemotsu." He it is who was the first ancestor of the U-kahi of Ata.

9th month, 5th day. The Emperor ascended to the peak of Mount Takakura in Uda, whence be had a prospect over all the land. On. Kuni-mi" Hill there were descried eighty bandits. Moreover, at the acclivity of Me-zaka there was posted an army of women, and at the acclivity of Wo-zaka "there was stationed a force of men. At the acclivity of Sumizaka was placed burning charcoal. This was the origin of the names Me-zaka, Wo-zaka, and Sumi-zaka.

Again there was the army of Ye-shiki, which covered all the village of Ihare. All the places occupied by the enemy were strong positions, and therefore the roads were cut off and obstructed, so that there was no room for passage. The Emperor, indignant at this, made prayer on that night in person, and then fell asleep. The Heavenly deity appeared to him in a dream, and instructed him, saying: "Take earth from within the shrine of the Heavenly Mount Kagu, and of it make eighty Heavenly platters. Also make sacred jars" and therewith sacrifice to the gods of Heaven and Earth. Moreover, pronounce a solemn imprecation. If thou doest so, the enemy will render submission of their own accord." The

Emperor received with reverence the directions given in his dream, and proceeded to carry them into execution.

Now Ukeshi the Younger again addressed the Emperor, saying: "There are in the province of Yamato, in the village of Shiki, eighty Shiki bandits. Moreover, in the village of Takawoliari (some say Katsuraki) there are eighty Akagane bandits. All these tribes intend to give battle to the Emperor, and thy servant is anxious in his own mind on his account. It were now good to take clay from the Heavenly fount Kagu, and therewith to make Heavenly platters with which to sacrifice to the gods of the Heavenly shrines and of the Earthly shrines. If after doing so, thou dost attack the enemy, they may be easily driven off." The Emperor, who had already taken the words of his dream for a good omen, When he now heard the words of Ukeshi the Younger was Still more pleased in his heart. He caused Shihi-netsu-hiko to put on ragged garments and a grass hat, and to disguise himself as an old man. He also caused Ukeshi the Younger to cover himself with a winnowing tray, so as to assume the appearance of an old woman, and then addressed them saying-: "Do ye two proceed to the Heavenly Mount Kagu, and secretly take earth from its summit. Having done so, return hither. By means of you I shall then divine whether my undertaking will be successful or not. Do your utmost and be watchful."

Now the enemy's army filled the road, and made all passage impossible. Then Shihi-netsu-hiko prayed, and said: "If it will be possible for our Emperor to conquer this land, let the road by which we must travel become open. But if not, let the brigands surely oppose our passage." Having thus spoken they set forth, and went straight onward. Now the hostile band, seeing the two men, laughed loudly, and said: "What an uncouth old man and old woman! "So with one accord they left the road, and allowed the two men to pass and proceed to the mountain, where they took the clay and returned with it. Hereupon the Emperor was greatly pleased, and with this clay he made eighty platters, eighty Heavenly small jars and sacred jars, with which he went up to the upper waters of the

River Nifu and sacrificed to the gods of Heaven and Earth. Immediately, on the Asahara plain by the river of Uda, it became as it were like foam on the water, the result of the curse cleaving to them.

Moreover, the Emperor went on to utter a vow, saying: "I will now make aMe n the eighty platters without using water. If the ame is formed, then shall I assuredly without effort and without recourse to the might of arms reduce the Empire to peace." So he made ame, which forthwith became formed of itself.

Again he made a vow, saving: "I will now take the sacred jars and sink thern in the River Nifu. If the fishes, whether great or small, become every one drunken and are carried down the stream, like as it were to floating maki leaves, then shall I assuredly succeed in establishing this land. But if this be not so, there will never be any result." Thereupon he sank the jars in the river with their mouths downward. After a while the fish all came to the surface, gaping and gasping as they floated down the stream. Then Shihi-netsu-hiko, seeing this, represented it to the Emperor, who was greatly rejoiced, and plucking up a five-hundred-branched masakaki tree of the upper waters of the River Nifu, be did worship therewith to all the gods. It was with this that the custom began of setting sacred jars.

At this time he commanded Michi no Omi no Mikoto, saying: "We are now in person" about to celebrate a public festival to Taka-mi-musubi no Mikoto, and I appoint thee Ruler of the festival, and grant thee the title of Idzu-hime. The earthen jars which are set up shall be called the Idzube, or sacred jars, the fire shall be called Idzu no Kagu-tsuchi, or sacred-fire-elder, the water shall be called Idzu no Midzuha no me, or sacred-water-female, the food shall be called Idzu-Uka no me, or sacred-food-female, the firewood shall be called Idzu no Yama-tsuchi, or sacred-mountain-elder, and the grass shall be called Idzu no No-tsuchi, or sacred-moor-elder."

Winter, 10th month, 1st day. The Emperor tasted the food of the Idzube, and arraying his troops set forth upon his march. He first of all attacked the eighty bandits at Mount Kunimi, routed and slew them. It was in this campaign that the Emperor, fully resolved on victory, made these verses, saying:

> Like the Shitadami
> Which creep around
> The great rock
> Of the Sea of Ise
> Where blows the divine wind—
> Like the Shitadami,
> My boys! my boys!
> We will creep around,
> And smite them utterly,
> And smite them utterly."

In this poem, by the great rock is intended the Hill of Kunimi.

After this the band which remained was still numerous, and their disposition could not be fathomed. So the Emperor privately commanded Michi no Omi no Mikoto, saying: "Do thou take with thee the Ohokume, and make a great muro at the village of Osaka. Prepare a copious banquet, invite the enemy to it, and then capture them." Michi no Omi no Mikoto thereupon, in obedience to the Emperor's secret behest, dug a muro at Osaka, and having selected his bravest soldiers, stayed therein mingled with the enemy. He secretly arranged with them, saying: "When they have got tipsy with sake, I will strike up a song. Do you, when you hear the sound of my song, all at the same time- stab the enemy." Having made this arrangement they took their seats, and the drinking-bout proceeded. The enemy, unaware that there was any plot, abandoned themselves to their feelings, and promptly became intoxicated. Then Michi no Omi no Mikoto struck up the following song:

> At Osaka
> In the great muro-house,

> Though men in plenty
> Enter and stay,
> We the glorious
> Sons of warriors,
> Wielding our mallet-heads,
> Wielding our stone-mallets,
> Will smite them utterly."

Now when our troops beard this song, they all drew at the same time their mallet-beaded swords, and simultaneously slew the enemy, so that there were no eaters left. The Imperial army were greatly delighted; they looked up to Heaven and laughed. Therefore he made a song, saying:

> Though folk say
> That one Yemishi
> Is a match for one hundred men
> They do not so much as resist."

The practise, according to which at the present time the Kume sing this and then laugh loud, had this origin.

Again he sang, saying:

> Ho now is the time;
> Ho! now is the time;
> Ha! Ha! Psha!
> Even now
> My boys!
> Even now
> My boys!"

All these songs were sung in accordance with the secret behest of the Emperor. He had not presumed to compose them of his own motion.

Then the Emperor said: "It is the part of a good general when victorious to avoid arrogance. The chief brigands have now been destroyed, but there are ten bands of villains of a similar stamp, who are disputatious. Their disposition can not be ascertained. Why should we remain for a long time in one place? By so doing we could not have control over emergencies." So he removed his camp to another place.

11th month, 7th day. The Imperial army proceeded in great force to attack the Hiko of Shiki. First of all the Emperor sent a messenger to summon Shiki the Elder, but he refused to obey. Again the Yata-garasu was sent to bring him. When the crow reached his camp it cried to him, saying: "The child of the Heavenly deity sends for thee. Haste! haste!" Shiki the Elder was enraged at this, and said: "Just when I heard that the conquering deity of Heaven was coming and was indignant at this, why shouldst thou, a bird of the crow tribe, utter such an abominable cry?" So be drew his bow and aimed at it. The crow forthwith fled away, and next proceeded to the house of Shiki the Younger, where it cried, saving: "The child of the Heavenly deity summons thee. Haste! haste! "Then Shiki the Younger was afraid, and, changing countenance, said: "Thy servant, hearing of the approach of the conquering deity of Heaven, is full of dread morning and evening. Well hast thou cried to me, O crow." He straightway made eight leaf-platters, on which he disposed food, and entertained the crow. Accordingly, in obedience to the crow he proceeded to the Emperor and informed him, saying: "My elder brother, Shiki the Elder, hearing of the approach of the child of the Heavenly deity, forthwith assembled eighty bandits and provided arms, with which he is about to do battle with thee. It will be well to take measures against him without delay." The Emperor accordingly assembled his generals and inquired of them, saying: "It appears that Shiki the Elder has now rebellious intentions. I summoned him, but again he will not come. What is to be done?" The generals said: "Shiki the Elder is a crafty knave.

It will be well, first of all, to send Shiki the Younger to make matters clear to him, and at the same time to make explanations to Kuraji the Elder and Kuraji the Younger. If after that they still refuse submission, it will not be too late to take warlike measures against them." Shiki the Younger was accordingly sent to explain to them their interests. But Shiki the Elder and the others adhered to their foolish design, and would not consent to submit. Then Shihi-netsu-hiko advised is follows: "Let us first send out our feebler troops by the Osaka road. When the enemy sees them he will assuredly proceed thither with all his best troops. We should then straightway urge forward our robust troops, and make straight For Sumi-zaka. Then with the water of the River Uda we should sprinkle the burning charcoal, and suddenly take them unawares, when they can not fail to be routed." The Emperor approved this plan, and sent out the feebler troops toward the enemy, who, thinking, that a powerful force was approaching, awaited them with all their power. Now up to this time, whenever the Imperial army attacked, they invariably caetured, and when they fought they were invariably victorious, so that the fighting men were all wearied out. Therefore the Emperor, to comfort the hearts of his leaders and men, struck off this verse:

> As we fight,
> Going forth and watching
> From between the trees
> Of Mount Inasa,
> We are famished.
> Ye keepers of cormorants
> (Birds of the island),
> Come now to our aid."

In the end he crossed Sumi-zaka with the stronger troops, and, going round by the rear, attacked them from two sides and put them to the rout, killing their chieftains Shiki the Elder and the others.

12th month, 4th day. The Imperial army at length attacked Naga-sune-hiko and fought with him repeatedly, but was unable to gain the victory. Then suddenly the sky became overcast, and hail fell. There appeared a wondrous kite of a golden color, which came flying and perched on the end of the Emperor's bow. The luster of this kite was of dazzling brightness, so that its appearance was like that of lightning. In consequence of this all Naga-sune-hiko's soldiers were dazzled and bewildered so that they could not fight stoutly.

Nagasune was the original name of the village, whence it became the name of a man. But in consequence of the lmperial army obtaining the favorable omen of the kite, the men of that time called it Tobi no mura. It is now called Tomi, which is a corruption of this.

Ever since Itsuse no Mikoto was hit by an arrow at the battle of Kusaka and died, the Emperor bore this in mind, and constantly cherished resentment for it. On this campaign it was his desire to, put all to death, and therefore he composed these verses, saying: "My mouth tingles

> With the ginger planted
> At the bottom of the hedge
> By the glorious Sons of warriors—

can not forget it;Let us smite them utterly. "Again he sang, saying:In the millet-field

> Is one stem of odorous garlic
> The glorious
> Sons of warriors
> Binding its stem

And binding its shoots Will smite it utterly. "Then again letting loose his army, he suddenly attacked him. In general, all these songs composed by the Emperor are termed kume uta, in allusion to the persons who took and sang them.

Now Naga-sune-hiko sent a foot-messenger, who addressed the Emperor, saying: "There was formerly a child of the Heavenly deity, who came down from Heaven to dwell here, riding in a Rock-boat of Heaven. His name was Kushi-dama Nigi-haya-hi no Mikoto. He took to wife my younger sister Mi-kashiki-ya-bime (also called Naga-sune-hime, or Tomi-ya-hime) of whom he at length had a child, named Umashi-ma-te no Mikoto. Therefore did I take Nigi-haya-hi no Mikoto for my lord, and did service to him. Can it be that there are two seeds of the children of the Heavenly deity? Why should any one else take the name of Child of the Heavenly deity and therewith rob people of their dominions? I have pondered this in my heart, but have as yet failed utterly to believe it." The Emperor said: "There are many other children of the Heavenly deity. If he whom thou hast taken as thy Lord were truly a child of the Heavenly deity, there would be surely some object which thou couldst show to us by way of proof." -Naga-sune-biko accordingly brought a single Heavenly-feathered-arrow of Nigihaya-hi no Mikoto, and a foot-quiver, and exhibited them respectfully to the Emperor. The Emperor examined them, and said: "These are genuine." Then in his turn he showed to Naga-sune-hiko the single Heavenly-feathered-arrow and quiver which he wore. When Naga-sune-hiko saw the Heavenly token be became more and more embarrassed. But the murderous weapons were already prepared, and things were in such a state that he was unable to pause in his career. Therefore be adhered to his misguided scheme, and would not alter his purpose.

Nigi-haya-hi no -Mikoto, knowing from the first that the Heavenly deity had simply generously bestowed the Empire on the Heavenly Grandchild, and that in view of the perverse disposition of Naga-sune it would be useless to instruct him in the relation of Heaven to Man, put him to death. He then came with his army and made submission. The

Emperor, who from the first had heard that Nigi-haya-hi no Mikoto had come down from Heaven, finding that he now had actually performed faithful service, accordingly praised him, and was gracious to him He was the ancestor of the Mono no Be House.

The year Tsuchi no to Hitsuji, Spring, 2nd month, 20th day. The Emperor commanded his generals to exercise the troops. At this time there were Tsuchi-gumo in three places, viz.: The Tohe of Nkihiki at Tada no Oka-zaki in the district of Sofu, the Kose Hofuri at Wani no Sakamoto and the Wi-Hofuri at Hosomi no Nagara no Okazaki. All of these, trusting to their valor, refused to present themselves at Court. The Emperor therefore sent detachments separately and put them all to death. There were, moreover, Tsuchi-gumo at the village of Taka-wohari, whose appearance was as follows: They had short bodies, and long arms and legs. They were of the same class as the pigmies. The Imperial troops wove nets of dolichos, which they flung over them and then slew them. Wherefore the name of that village was changed to Katsuraki. It is in the land of Ihare. Its ancient name was Kataru, or Katatachi. When our Imperial forces routed the enemy, a great army assembled and filled that country. Its name was accordingly changed to Ihare.

Another account says that when the Emperor on a previous occasion tasted the food of the sacred jars, he moved forward his army on an expedition toward the West. At this time the eighty bandits of Katsuraki were encamped together there. A great battle with the Emperor followed, and they were at length destroyed by the Imperial army. Therefore that place was called the village of Ihare. Again, the place where the Imperial troops made a warlike stand was called Takeda. The place where he built a castle was named Kita. Moreover, the place where the enemy fell in battle, their dead bodies prostrate, with their forearms for pillows, was called Tsura-maki-da.

The Emperor, in Autumn, the 9th month of the previous year, secretly took clay of the Heavenly Mount Kagu, with which he made eighty platters, and thereafter performing abstinence in person, sacrificed to all the gods. He was thereby at length enabled to establish the world in peace. Therefore he called the place where the clay was taken Haniyasu.

3rd month, 7th day. The Emperor made an order, saying: "During the six years that our expedition against the East has lasted, owing to my reliance on the Majesty of Imperial Heaven, the wicked bands have met death. It is true that the frontier lands are still unpurified, and that a remnant of evil is still refractory. But in the region of the Central Land there is no more wind and dust. Truly we should make a vast and spacious capital, and plan it great and strong.

"At present things are in a crude and obscure condition, and the people's minds are unsophisticated. They roost in nests or dwell in eaves . Their manners are simply what is customary. Now if a great man were to establish laws, justice could not fail to flourish. And even if some gain should accrue to the people, in what way would this interfere with the Sage's action? Moreover, it will be well to open up and clear the mountains and forests, and to construct a palace. Then I may reverently assume the Precious Dignity, and so give peace to my good subjects. Above, I should then respond to the kindness of the Heavenly Powers in granting me the Kingdom, and below, I should extend the line of the Imperial descendants and foster right-mindedness. Thereafter the capital may be extended so as to embrace all the six cardinal points, and the eight cords may be covered so as to form a roof. Will this not be well?

"When I observe the Kashiha-hara plain, which lies southwest of Mount Unebi, it seems the Center of the Land. I must set it in order."

Accordingly he in this month commanded officers to set about the construction of an Imperial Residence.

(661 B.C.) Year Kanoye Saru, Autumn, 8th month, 16th day. The Emperor, intending to appoint a wife, sought afresh children of noble families. Now there was a man who made representation to him, saying: "There is a child who was born to Koto-shiro-nushi no Kami by his union with Tama-kushi-hime, daughter of Mizo-kuhi-ni no Kami of Mishima. Her name is Hime-tatara-i-suzu-hime no Amikoto. She is a woman of

remarkable beauty." The Emperor was rejoiced, and on the 24th day of the 9th month be received Hime-tatara-i-suzu-hime no Mikoto and made her his wife.

(660 B.C.) Year Kanoto Tori, Spring, 1st month 1st day. The Emperor assumed the Imperial Dignity in the Palace of Kashiha-bara. This year is reckoned the first year of his reign. He honored his wife by making her Empress. The children born to him by her were Kami-ya-wi-mimi no Mikoto and Kami-nunagaba mimi -no Mikoto.

Therefore there is an ancient saying in praise of this, as follows: "In Kashiha-bara in Unebi, he mightily established his palace-pillars on the foundation of the bottom-rock, and reared aloft the cross roof-timbers to the Plain of High Heaven. The name of the Emperor who thus began to rule the Empire was Kami Yamato Ihare-biko Hohodemi."

On the day on which he first began the Heavenly institution, Michi no Omi no Mikoto, the ancestor of the Ohotomo House, accompanied by the Oho-kume Be, was enabled, by means of a secret device received from the Emperor, to use incantations and magic formulas so as to dissipate evil influences. The use of magic formulas had its origin from this.

2nd year, Spring, 2nd month, 2nd day. The Emperor ascertained merit and dispensed rewards. To Michi no Omi no Mikoto he granted a site for a house in which to dwell at the village of Tsuki-zaka, thereby showing him special favor.

Moreover, he caused the Oho-kume to dwell at a place on the river-bank, west of Mount Unebi, now called Kume no Mura. Such was the origin of this name. Utsu-hiko was made Miyakko of the land of Yamato. Moreover, he gave to Ukeshi the younger the village of Takeda, constituting him Agata-nushi of Takeda. He was the ancestor of the Mohi-tori of Uda. Shiki the younger, whose personal name was Kuro-haya, was made Agata-nushi of Shiki. Moreover, he appointed a man called Tsune to be Miyakko of the Land of Katsuraki. The Yata-garasu was also included in the ranks of those who received rewards. His descendants are the Agata-nushi of Katsurano and the Tonomori Be.

(657 B.C.) 4th year, Spring, 2nd month, 23rd day. The Emperor issued the following decree: "The spirits of our Imperial ancestors reflecting their radiance down from Heaven, illuminate and assist us. All our enemies have now been subdued, and there is peace within the seas. We ought to take advantage of this to perform sacrifice to the Heavenly deities, and therewith develop filial duty."

He accordingly established spirit-terraces amongst the Tomi hills, which were called Kami-tsu-wono no Kaki-hara. Shimo-tsu-wono no Kaki-hara. There he worshiped his Imperial ancestors, the Heavenly deities.

(630 B.C.) 31st year, Summer, 4th month, 1st day. The Imperial palanquin made a circuit, in the course of which the Emperor ascended the Hill Waki Kamu no Hotsuma. Here, having viewed the shape of the land on all sides, he said: "Oh! what a beautiful country we have become possessed of! Though a blessed land of inner-tree-fiber, yet it resembles a dragon-fly licking its hinder parts." From this it first received the name of Akitsu-shima.

Of old, Izanagi no Mikoto, in naming this country, said: Yamato is the land of Ura-yasu: it is the land of Hosohoko no Chi-taru: it is is the land of Shiwa-Kami-Ho-tsuma."

Afterward Oho-namuchi no Oho-kami named it the land of Tama-gaki no Uchi-tsu-kuni.

Finally, when Nigi-haya-hi no Mikoto soared across the Great Void in a Heaven-rock-boat, be espied this region and descended upon it. Therefore he gave it a name and called it Sora-mitsu-Yamato.

42nd year, Spring, 1st month, 3rd day. He appointed Prince Kami-nunagaha-mimi -no Mikoto Prince Imperial.

76th year, Spring, 3rd month, 11th day. The Emperor died in the palace of Kashiba-bara. His age was then 127. The following year, Autumn, the 12th day of the 9th month, be was buried in the Misasagi, northeast of Mount Unebi.

THE LAWS OF ROTOKU TENNO

BOOK XXV

HE EMPEROR AME-YORODZU TOYO-HI

The Emperor Ame-yorodzu toyo-hi honored the religion of Buddha and despised the Way of the Gods (as is instanced by his cutting down the trees of the shrine of Iku-kuni-dama). He was of a gentle disposition, and loved men of learning. He made no distinction of noble and mean, and continually dispensed beneficent edicts.

At this time Ohotomo no Nagatoko no Muraji (his cognomen was Mumakahi), girt with a golden quiver, stood on the right hand of the throne, and Intigami no Takebe no Kimi, girt with a golden quiver, stood on the left hand of the throne. The functionaries, Omi, Muraji, Kuni no Miyakko, Tomo no Miyakko and the 180 Be, ranged in order, went round making obeisance. On this day, the title of Ko-so-bo was conferred on the Empress Toyo-takara, and Naka no Ohoye was made Prince Imperial, Abe no Uchimaro no Omi was made Sa-dai-jin, and Soga no Kurayamada Ishikaba no Maro no Omi was made U-dai-jin. A great brocade cap of honor was given to Nakatomi no Kamako no Muraji, and he was made Naijin with an increased feudal revenue of a large number of houses, etc., etc. Nakatomi no Kamako no Muraji cherished the most sincere loyalty. Trusting to his power as ruling Minister, he took place over the various functionaries. In respect therefore to advancements and dismissals, taking measures or abandoning them, everything was done in accordance with his counsel, etc., etc. The Buddhist priest Min Hoshi and Kuromaro Takamuko no Fubito were made national doctors.

19th day. The Emperor, the Empress Dowager, and the Prince Imperial summoned together the Ministers under the great tsuki tree, and made an oath appealing to the gods of Heaven and Earth, and saying:

"Heaven covers us: Earth upbears us: the Imperial way is but one. But in this last degenerate age, the order of Lord and Vassal was destroyed, until Supreme Heaven by Our hands put to death the traitors. Now, from this time forward, both parties shedding their hearts' blood, the Lord will eschew double methods of government, and the Vassal will avoid duplicity in his service of the sovereign! On him who breaks this oath, Heaven will send a curse and earth a plague, demons will slay them, and men will smite them. This is as manifest as the sun and moon."

The style 4th year of the Empress Ame-toyo-takara ikashi-hi tarashi-hime was altered to Daikwa, 1st year.

(645 A.D.) Daikwa, 1st year, Autumn, 8th month, 5th day. Governors of the Eastern provinces were appointed. Then the Governors were addressed as follows: "In accordance with the charge entrusted to Us by the gods of Heaven, We propose at this present for the first time to regulate the myriad provinces.

"When you proceed to your posts, prepare registers of all the free subjects of the State and of the people under the control of others, whether great or small. Take account also of the acreage of cultivated land. As to the profits arising from the gardens and ponds, the water and land, deal with them in common with the people. Moreover, it is not competent for the provincial Governors, while in their provinces, to decide criminal cases, nor are they permitted by accepting bribes to bring the people to poverty and misery. When they come up to the capital they must not bring large numbers of the people in their train. They are only allowed to bring with them the Kuni no Miyakko and the district officials. But when they travel on public business they may ride the horses of their

-department, and eat the food of their department. From the rank of Suke upward those who obey this law will surely be rewarded, while those who disobey it shall be liable to be reduced in cap-rank. On all, from the rank of Hangwan downward, who accept bribes a fine shall imposed of double the amount, and they shall eventually be punished criminally according to the greater or less heinousness of the case. Nine men are allowed as attendants on a Chief Governor, seven on an assistant, and five on a secretary. If this limit is exceeded, and they are accompanied by a greater number, both chief and followers shall be punished criminally.

"If there be any persons who lay claim to a title, but who, not being Kuni no Miyakko, Tonio no Miyakko, or Inaki of districts by descent, unscrupulously draw up lying memorials, saying: 'From the time of our forefathers we have had charge of this Miyake or have ruled this district'— in such cases, ye, the Governors, must not readily make application to the Court in acquiescence in such fictions, but must ascertain particularly the true facts before making your report.

"Moreover, on waste pieces of ground let arsenals be erected, and let the swords and armor, with the bows and arrows of the provinces and districts, be deposited together in them. In the case of the frontier provinces which border close on the Yemishi, let all the weapons be mustered together, and let them remain in the hands of their original owners. In regard to the six districts of the province of Yamato, let the officials who are sent there prepare registers of the population, and also take an account of the acreage of cultivated land. (This means to examine the acreage of the cultivated ground, and the numbers, houses, and ages of the people.)

"Ye Governors of provinces, take careful note of this and withdraw." Accordingly presents were made them of silk and cloth, which varied in the case of each person."

This day a bell and box were provided in the Court .The Emperor issued an order, saying: "If there be a complainant, in case the person in question belongs to a Tomo no Miyak-ko, let the Tomo no Miyakko first make inquiry and then report to Us. In case the person in question has an elder, let the elder first make inquiry and then report to Us. If, however, the Tomo no Miyakko or the elder does not come to a clear decision respecting the complaint, let a document be received and placed in the box, and punishment will be inflicted according to the offense. The person who receives the document should at dawn take it and make report to the Inner Palace, when We will mark on it the year and month, and communicate it to the Ministers. In case there is any neglect to decide it, or if there are malpractises on the part of intriguing persons, let the complainant strike the bell. This is why the bell is hung and box provided in the Court. Let the people of the Empire know and appreciate Our intention.

"Moreover, the law of men and women shall be that the children born of a free man and a free woman shall belong to the father: if a free man takes to wife a slave woman, her children shall belong to the mother: if a free woman marries a slave man, the children of the marriage shall belong to the father; if they are slaves of two houses, the children shall belong to the mother. The children of temple-serfs shall follow the rule for freemen. But in regard to others who become slaves, they shall be treated according to the rule for slaves. Do ye now publish this well to the people as a beginning of regulations."

8th day. A messenger was sent to the Great Temple to summon together the Buddhist priests and nuns, and to address them on the part of the Emperor, saying: "In the 13th year of the reign of the Emperor who ruled the world in the Palace of Shikishima, King Myong of Pekche reverently transmitted the Law of Buddha to our great Yamato. At this time the Ministers in a body were opposed to its transmission. Only Soga no Iname no Sukune believed in this Law, and the Emperor accordingly instructed him to receive it with reverence. In the reign of the Emperor who ruled the world in the Palace of Wosada, Soga no Mumako no Sukune, influenced by the reverence for his deceased father, continued to prize highly the doctrines of Buddha. But the other Ministers had no faith in it, and its institutes had almost perished when the Emperor instructed Miamako no Sukune reverently to receive this Law. In the reign of the Empress who ruled the world in the Palace of Woharida, Mumako no Sukune, on behalf of the Empress, made an embroidered figure of Buddha sixteen feet high and a copper image of Buddha sixteen feet high. He exalted the doctrine of Buddha and showed honor to its priests and nuns. It is Our desire anew to exalt the pure doctrine and brilliantly to promulgate great principles. We therefore appoint as professors the following ten persons: The S'ramana, Poknyang, Hye-un, Syang-an, Nyong-un, and Hye-chi, Taihoshi of Koma, and Sobin, Doto, Yerin, Yemyo and Yeon, chief priests of temples. We separately appoint the Hoshi, Yemyo, chief priest of the Temple of Kudara.

"Let these ten professors well instruct the priests in general the practise of the teachings of Shaka. It is needful that they be made to comply with the Law. If there is a difficulty about repairing temples built by any from the Emperor down to the Tomo no Miyakko, We will in all cases assist in doing so. We shall also cause Temple Commissioners and Chief Priests to be appointed, who shall make a circuit to all the temples, and having ascertained the actual facts respecting the priests and nuns, their male and female slaves, and the acreage of their cultivated lands, report all the particulars clearly to us."

19th day. Commissioners were sent to all the provinces to take a record of the total numbers of the people. The Emperor on this occasion made an edict, as follows:

"In the times of all the Emperors, from antiquity downward, subjects have been set apart for the purpose of making notable their reigns and banding down their names to posterity. Now the Omi and Muraji, the Tomo no Miyakko and the Kuni no Miyakko, have each one set apart their own vassals, whom they compel to labor at their arbitrary pleasure. Moreover, they cut off the hills and seas, the woods and plains, the ponds and rice-fields belonging to the provinces and districts, and appropriate them to themselves. Their contests are never-ceasing. Some engross to themselves many tens of thousands of shiro of rice-land, while others possess in all patches of ground too small to stick a needle into. When the time comes for the payment of taxes, the Omi, the Muraji, and the Tomo no Miyakko first collect them for themselves and then band over a share. In the case of repairs to palaces or the construction of misasagi, they each bring their own vassals, and do the work according to circumstances. The Book of Changes says: 'Diminish that which is above: increase that which is below: if measures are framed according to the regulations, the resources of the State suffer no injury, and the people receive no hurt.'

"At the present time, the people are still few. And yet the powerful cut off portions of land and water and converting them into private ground, sell it to the people, demanding the price yearly. From this time forward the sale of land is not allowed. Let no man without due authority make himself a landlord, engrossing to himself that which belongs to the helpless."

The people were greatly rejoiced.

Winter, 12th month, 9th day. The Emperor removed the capital to Toyosaki in Nagara at Naniha. Old people, remarking upon this to one another, said: "The movement of rats toward Naniha from spring until summer was an omen of the removal of the capital."

24th day. It was reported from the land of Koshi: "Driftwood of the seashore passed away toward the east, leaving an impression on the sand like a plowed rice-field in appearance."

This year was the year Kinoto Mi (42nd) of the Cycle.

2nd year, Spring, 1st month, 1st day. As soon as the ceremonies of the new year's congratulations were over the Emperor promulgated an edict of reforms, as follows:

"I. Let the people established by the ancient Emperors, etc., as representatives of children be abolished, also the Miyake of various places and the people owned as serfs by the Wake, the Omi, the Muraji, the Tomo no Miyakko, the kuni no Miyakko and the Mura no Obito. Let the farmsteads in various places be abolished." Consequently fiefs were granted for their sustenance to those of the rank of Daibu and upward on a descending scale. Presents of cloth and silk stuffs were given to the officials and people, varying in value.

"Further We say. It is the business of the Daibu to govern the people. If they discharge this duty thoroughly, the people have trust in them, and an increase of their revenue is therefore for the good of the people.

"II. The capital is for the first time to be regulated, and Governors appointed for the Home provinces and districts.

"Let barriers, outposts, guards, and post-horses, both special and ordinary, be provided, bell-tokens made, and mountains and rivers regulated.

For each ward in the capital let there be appointed one alderman, and for four wards one chief alderman Who shall be charged with the superintendence of the population, and the examination of criminal matters. For appointment as chief aldermen of wards let men be taken belonging to the wards, of unblemished character, firm and upright, so that they may fitly sustain the duties of the time. For appointments as aldermen, whether of rural townships or of city wards, let ordinary subjects be taken belonging to the township or ward, of good character and solid capacity. If such men are not to be found in the township or ward in question, it is permitted to select and employ men of the adjoining township or ward.

"The Home provinces shall include the region from the River Yokogaha at Nabari on the east, from Mount Senoyama in Kii on the south, from Kushibuchi in Akashi on the west, and from Mount Afusaka-yama in Sasanami in Afumi on the north. Districts of forty townships are constituted Greater Districts, of from thirty to four townships are constituted Middle Districts, and of three or fewer townships are constituted Lesser Districts. For the district authorities, of whatever class, let there be taken Kuni no Miyakko of unblemished character, such as may fitly sustain the duties of the time and made Tairei and Shorei.

Let men of solid capacity and intelligence who are skilled in writing and arithmetic be appointed assistants and clerks.

"The number of special or ordinary post-horses given shall in all cases follow the number of marks on the posting bell-tokens. When bell-tokens are given to officials of the provinces and barriers, let them be held in both cases by the chief official, or in his absence by the assistant official.

"III. Let there now be provided for the first time registers of population, books of account and a system of the receipt and regranting of distribution-land .

"Let every fifty houses be reckoned a township, and in every township let there be one alderman who shall be charged with the superintendence of the population the direction of the sowing of crops and the cultivation of mulberry-trees, the prevention and examination of offenses, and the enforcement of the payment of taxes and of forced labor.

"For rice-land, thirty paces in length by twelve paces in breadth shall be reckoned a tan. Ten tan make one cho. For each tan the tax is two sheaves and two bundles (such as can be grasped in the hand) of rice; for each cho the tax is twenty-two sheaves of rice. On mountains or in valleys where the land is precipitous, or in remote places where the population is scanty, such arrangements are to be made as may be convenient.

"IV. The old taxes and forced labor are abolished, and a system of commuted taxes instituted. These shall consist of fine silks, coarse silks, raw silk and floss silk, all in accordance with what is produced in the locality. For each cho of rice-land the rate is one rod of fine silk, or for four cho one piece forty feet in length by two and a half feet in width. For coarse silk the rate is two rods (per cho), or one piece for every two cho of the same length and width as the fine silk. For cloth the rate is four rods of the same dimensions as the fine and coarse silk, i.e., one tan for each cho. (No rates of weight are anywhere given for silk or floss silk.) Let there be levied separately a commuted house tax. All houses shall pay each one rod and two feet of cloth. The extra articles of this tax, as well as salt and offerings, will depend on what is produced in the locality. For horses for the public service, let every hundred houses contribute one horse of medium quality. Or if the horse is of superior quality, let one be contributed by every two hundred houses. If the horses have to be purchased, the price shall be made up by a payment from each house of one rod and two feet of cloth. As to weapons, each person shall contribute a sword, armor, bow and arrows, a flag, and a drum. For coolies, the old system, by which one coolie was provided by every thirty houses, is altered, and one coolie is to be furnished from every fifty houses (one is for employment as a menial servant) for allotment to the various functionaries. Fifty houses shall be allotted to provide rations for one coolie, and one house shall contribute two rods and two feet of cloth and five masu of rice in lieu of service.

For waiting-women in the Palace, let there be furnished the sisters or daughters of district officials of the rank of Shorei or upward - good-looking women (with one male and two female servants to attend on them), and let 100 houses be allotted to provide rations for one waiting-woman.

The cloth and rice supplied in lieu of service shall, in every case, follow the same rule as for coolies."

In this month the Emperor occupied the separate Palace of Koshiro. He sent messengers to command the provinces and districts to repair the arsenals. Yemishi came and did homage.

One book says: "The Miyake of Kosbiro, in the village of Sayabe, at Naniba, was pulled dowm, and a temporary Palace erected."

2nd month, 15th day. The Emperor proceeded to the Eastern Gate of the Palace, where, by Soga, Oho-omi of the Right, he decreed as follows:

"The God Incarnate, the Emperor Yamato-neko, who rules the world, gives command to the Ministers assembled in his presence, to the Omi, Muraji, Kuni no Miyakko, Tomo no Miyakko, and subjects of various classes, saying:

"We are informed that wise rulers of the people bung a bell at their gate, and so took cognizance of the complaints of their subjects; they erected buildings in the thoroughfares, where they listened to the censures of the passers-by. Even the opinions of the grass and firewood gatherers they inquired personally and used for their guidance. We, therefore, on a former occasion, made an edict, saying: 'In ancient times the Empire was ruled by having at the Court flags of honor for the encouragement of good, and a board of censure, the object being to diffuse principles of Government and to invite remonstrances.' All this served widely to ascertain the opinions of those below. Kwan-Tsze said:

The Emperor Hwang by establishing the Conferences of the Bright Hall, observed the opinions of the wise on the upper hand, while the Emperor Yao, having the inquiries of the street-houses, listened to the people on the lower hand. Shun again had flags to proclaim merit and thus secure publicity; and Yu set up a drum at his Court, thus providing for the investigation into expectations. Thang had the Court of the general control of Districts, whereby he observed the faults of the people. King Wu had the park of the Spirit terrace, and therefore the wise had advancement. Thus the sage Emperor and Illustrious Sovereigns of antiquity possessed and did not lose; they gained and did not destroy.'

"The object of hanging up a bell, of providing a box, and of appointing a man to receive petitions, is to make those who have grievances or remonstrances deposit their petitions in the box. The receivers of petitions are commanded to make their report to Us every morning. When We receive this report We shall draw the attention of the Ministers to it, and cause them to consider it, and We trust that this may be done without delay. But if there should be neglect on the part of the Ministers, and a want of diligence or partisan intrigues, and if We, moreover, should refuse to listen to remonstrance, let the complainant strike the bell. There has been already an Imperial command to this effect. But some time afterward there was a man of intelligence and uprightness who, cherishing in his heart the spirit of a national patriot, addressed Us a memorial of earnest remonstrance, which he placed in the box prepared for the purpose. We therefore now publish it to the black-haired people here assembled. This memorial runs as follows: 'Those subjects who come to the capital in connection with the discharge of their duty to the Government of the Country, are detained by the various public functionaries and put to forced labor of various kinds, etc., etc.' We are still moved with strong sympathy by this. How could the people expect that things would come to this? Now no long time has elapsed since the capital was removed, so that so far from being at home, we are, as it were, strangers. It is therefore impossible to avoid employing the people, and they have therefore been, against Our will, compelled to labor. As often as Our minds dwell on this We have never been able to sleep in peace. When We saw this memorial we could not refrain from a joyous exclamation. We have accordingly complied with the language of remonstrance, and have put a stop to the forced services at various places.

"In a former edict, We said: 'Let the man who remonstrates sign his name.' Those who disobey this injunction are doubtless actuated by a wish to serve their country, and not by a desire of personal gain. Whether a man signs his name or not, let him not fail to remonstrate with Us on Our neglect or forgetfulness."

Another edict was made as follows: "There are many things of which the assembled people of the land complain. We are now about to explain our principles. Listen attentively to what We say. Those who come to the capital and assemble at Court in order to obtain decisions of doubtful points should not disperse in the morning, but remain together in attendance at Court."

Koryo, Pekche, Imna, and Silla all together sent envoys to offer tribute.

22nd day. The Emperor returned from the detached Palace of Koshiro.

3rd month, 2nd day. An edict was issued to the Governors of the Eastern provinces, saying: "Do all ye Ministers and Daibu assembled in attendance on Us, as well as ye Omi, Muraji, Kuni no Miyakko, and Tomo no Miyakko, and also ye subjects of every class, listen to this: He that is lord between Heaven and Earth and rules the myriad people ought not to exercise control alone: be must have Ministers to support him. From generation to generation, therefore, Our Imperial ancestors have governed along with the ancestors of you, My Ministers. It is Our wish also, with the protecting power of the Gods, to associate you with Ourselves in the government. We therefore, on a former occasion, appointed Daibu, of good family, to the government of the eight Eastern provinces. Then the Governors went to their posts. Six obeyed the laws, and two were regardless of Our commands. In each case censure or praise became audible. We thereupon commended those who kept the law, and were severe with those who disregarded the instructions given them. He that would be a ruler, whether he be Lord or Minister, should first correct himself, and then correct others. If he do not correct himself, how shall he be able to correct others? He therefore who does not correct himself, be he Lord or be he Minister, will meet with calamity. Should one not be watchful? If ye, the leaders, are upright, who shall presume to be otherwise? Do ye now be guided by Our former commands in dispensing your judgments."

19th day. The Emperor made a decree to the Choshushi of the Eastern provinces, saying:

"Hear this, all ye Ministers and Daibu assembled in Our presence, as well as ye Kuni no Miyakko and Tomo no Miyakko, together with the subjects of all classes! In the 8th month of last year, We in person admonished you, saving: 'Do not use your official authority to appropriate public or private property: you should consume food of your own domain, and ride horses of your own domain. Those who disregard this admonition, if of the rank of Assistant Governor or higher, shall be degraded in official rank, if of the rank of Clerk or lower, shall be sentenced to flogging. Those who convert property to their own use shall be mulcted in double its value.' Such was the edict which We issued.

Now, when We inquired from the Choshushi and the Miyakko of the various provinces whether the local Governors, when they proceeded to their posts, attended to this admonition or not, the Choshushi and the others informed Us fully of the facts, to wit: The offense of Kuhi, Hodzumi no Omi, consists in having made exactions from each family among the people, and though he repented and gave back the things, not doing so completely. His two assistants, Fuse no Omi and Shidamu, Kose no Omi, have offended by not correcting the error of their chief, etc., etc. The inferior officials have all been guilty of offenses. The offense of Kose no Tokune no Omi consists in having made exactions from each family among the people, and though he repented and returned the things, not doing so completely. He has, moreover, taken away the horses of the agricultural serfs. His two assistants, Yenowi no Muraji and Oshizaka no Muraji, did not correct the faults of their chief, but on the contrary joined with him in prosecuting their own advantage. They have, moreover, taken away horses belonging to the Kuni no Miyakko. Sumi, Utena no Atahe, although at first he remonstrated with his chief, yet at last became corrupt along with him. The inferior officials are all guilty of offenses. The offense of Ki no Marikida no Omi consists in having sent men to Asakura no Kimi and Winouhe [Inouye] no Kimi to fetch their horses for him to look at. Further, he made Asakura no Kimi manufacture swords. Further, be got from Asakura no Kimi his bow-cloth. Further, he did not honestly return to their owners the articles sent by the Kuni no Miyakko in lieu of weapons, but delivered them to the Kuni no Miyakko in an irregular manner. Further, in the province committed to his charge, he allowed himself to be robbed of a sword. Further, in the province of Yamato he allowed himself to be robbed of a sword. These are the offenses of Ki no Omi and of his assistants, Obo-guchi, Miwa no Kimi, and Momoyori, Kahabe no Omi. Their subordinate officials, Shibatsu, Kahabe no Omi, Tajibi no Fukame, Mozu no Nagaye, Katsuraki no Saigusa, Naniha no Kubikame, Tnukabi no Isogimi, Maro, Iki no Fubito, Tajihi no Inume; these eight persons, all are guilty of offenses. The offense of Adzumi no Muraji consists in this-that when Wadoku no Fubito was ill, he caused the Kuni no Miyakko to send him government property. Further, he took horses belonging to the Yube. The offense of his assistant Momoyori, Kashihade no Omi, consists in his having received and stored in his house articles paid in lieu of hay. Further, he took the horses of the Kuni no Miyakko and exchanged them for others. The two brothers, Ihatsutsu and Yumaro, Kahabe no Omi, have also been guilty of offenses. Ohochi no Muraji's offense consists in his having disobeyed Our former decree, which was as follows: 'Let not the local Governors personally judge the plaints of the people in the districts placed under their charge.' He has disobeyed this edict in that he has taken it upon himself personally to judge the plaints of the men of Udo, and the matter of the slaves of Nakatomi no Toko. Nakatomi no Toko is equally guilty with him in this matter. The offense of Kisbida no Omi consists in his having bad his official sword stolen when he was in the province of Yamato. This showed a want of circumspection. As for Womidori no Omi and Tamba no Omi, they have been simply incompetent, but not guilty of anv offense. The two men, Imbe no Konomi and Mutsuki, Nakatomi no Ifuraji, have also been guilty of offenses. Neither of these two men viz., Hada no Omi and Taguchi no Omi. has committed any offense. The offense of Heguri no Omi consists in his having neglected to investigate the plaints of the men of Mikuni. Upon a review of these facts we find that all this is owing to the neglect and incompetence of you three, viz., Ki no Mariki no Omi, Kose no Tokune no Omi, and Hodzumi no Kuhi no Omi. Is it not painful to Us to think of your disobedience to Our edict? Now if he who has pastoral care of the people, whether as Lord or Minister, gives a personal example of upright conduct, who shall presume to do otherwise? But if he, whether Lord or Minister, be not upright in heart, it is fit that he should bear the guilt. What avails it to repent afterward? We shall therefore consider the cases of all these local Governors and punish them according to the gravity of their offenses.

"With regard, moreover, to the Kuni no Miyakko who have disobeyed Our edict by sending presents to the Governors of their provinces, and, at length joining with them in the pursuit of gain, constantly conceive foul wickedness, repressive measures are indispensable. But although such are Our thoughts, we have only begun to occupy our new palace, and are about to make offerings to all the Kami, both which matters belong to the present year. Moreover, it is not meet to employ the people in labor during the months of agriculture. But in connection with the building of a new palace, it was decidedly impossible to avoid doing so. Deeply conscious of both these considerations, We proclaim a general amnesty throughout the Empire. From this time forward, let the local Governors of provinces and districts be zealous and do their utmost. Let them avoid profligacy. Let messengers be sent to release all banished men of the various provinces, and all prisoners in the gaols without exception.

In contradistinction from the rest, the following six men, viz., Shihoya no Konoshiro, Kamikozo no Saigusa, Asakura no Kimi, Mariko no Muraji, Mikaba no Oho-tomo noAtabe and Suzuki wo no Atabe, have been obedient to the Emperor. We profoundly commend their sentiments.

"Let the official rice-fields belonging to the public offices in various places be done away with, as well as the lent-rice in various places belonging to the Ko-so-bo Kibishima and let her official rice-lands be distributed among all Our Ministers and Tomo no Miyakko. Moreover, let rice-land and hill-tracts be given to those temples which are omitted from the registers."

20th day. The Prince Imperial, by a messenger, addressed a petition to the Emperor, saying: "In the reigns of the former Emperors, they treated the Empire as a whole, and so ruled it. But, when we come to the present time, there was division and separation, to the injury of the Work (the work of the State is meant). Now that it has devolved on the Emperor our Sovereign to have pastoral charge of the myriad people, Heaven and Man respond harmoniously to each other and the government has been reformed I, therefore, filled with joy and veneration, place it on my head, and prostrating myself, address Your Majesty: 'The Emperor who now rules the Land of the Eight Islands as an Incarnate Deity inquired of thy servant, saying: "Should the Kosbiro no Iribe in the possession of Ministers, Muraji, Tomo no -Miyakko, Kuni no Miyakko, and established in the days of former Emperors, the Mina no Iribe in the private possession of Imperial Princes, and the Mina no Iribe belonging to the Imperial Father 78 Ohoye (Hikobito Obove is meant), as well as their Miyake, be allowed to remain the same as in former generations, or not?" Thy servant having received this command with reverence, replies respectfully, saying: "In Heaven there are not two suns: in a country there are not two rulers. It is therefore the Emperor alone who is supreme over all the Empire, and who has a right to the services of the myriad people. Make a special selection of laborers from the Iribe and from the people granted in fee, and follow the former arrangement. For the rest, it may be feared that they will be put to forced labor on private authority. I therefore offer to the Emperor 524 men of the Iribe, and 181 Miyake."

22nd day. The Emperor made a decree, as follows: "We are informed that a Prince of the Western Land admonished his people, saying: 'Those who made interments in ancient times resorted to a high ground which they formed into a tomb. They did not pile up a mound, nor did they plant trees. The inner and outer coffin were merely enough to last till the bones decayed, the shroud was merely sufficient to last till the flesh decayed. I shall therefore cultivate the unproductive pieces of land occupied by these tombs, to the end that their place may be forgotten after changing generations. Deposit not in them gold or silver or copper or iron, and let earthenware objects alone represent the clay chariots and straw figures of antiquity. Let the interstices of the coffin be varnished. Let the offerings consist of rice presented three times, and let not pearls or jewels be placed in the mouth of the deceased. Bestow not jewel-shirts or jade armor. All these things are practises of the unenlightened vulgar.' Again it is said: 'Burial is putting away, and proceeds from the desire to prevent the dead from being seen by people.' Of late, the poverty of our people is absolutely owing to the construction of tombs. We now issue regulations making distinction of noble and mean.

"The inner dimensions of tombs of persons of the rank of Princes and upward shall be nine feet in length by five in width. Their outer limits shall be nine fathoms square and their height five fathoms. The work shall be completed by 1000 laborers in seven days. At the time of interment white cloth shall be used for the hangings of the bier, etc. A hearse may be used.

"The inner dimensions of tombs of Superior Ministers shall be similar in length, breadth, and height to the above. Their outer limits shall be seven fathoms square, and they shall be three fathoms in height." The work shall be completed by 500 laborers in five days. At the time of interment white cloth shall be used for the hangings of the bier, which shall be borne on men's shoulders.

"The inner dimensions of a tomb of a Minister of a lower class shall be in every respect similar in length, breadth, and height to the above. Their outer limits shall be five fathoms square, and they shall be two and a half fathoms in height. The work shall be completed by 250 laborers in three days. At the time of interment white cloth shall be used for hangings. In other matters the same rule as before is to be followed.

"The inner dimensions of the tombs of persons of the rank of Dainin and Shonin shall be nine feet in length and four feet in height and breadth. The ground shall be made level and no mound raised. The work shall be completed by 100 laborers in one day.

"In the case of persons from the rank of Dairei to that of Shochi inclusive, the tombs shall in all respects follow the rule of Dainin, but the work shall be completed by fifty laborers in one day.

"Let small stones be used for the tombs of all from the rank of Prince down to that of Shochi, and let white cloth be used for the hangings.

"When ordinary persons die, let them be buried in the ground, and let the hangings be of coarse cloth. Let the interment not be delayed for a single day.

"The construction of places of temporary interment is not allowed in any case, from Princes down to common people.

"Not only in the Home provinces, but in the provinces generally, let plots of ground be set apart for interments. It is not permitted to pollute the earth by dispersed interments in various places.

"When a man dies, there have been cases of people sacrificing themselves by strangulation, or of strangling others by way of sacrifice, or of compelling the dead man's horse to be sacrificed, or of burying valuables in the grave in honor of the dead, or of cutting off the hair, and stabbing the thighs and pronouncing a eulogy on the dead (while in this condition). Let all such old customs be entirely discontinued.

"A certain book says: 'No gold or silver, no silk brocades, and no colored stuffs are to be buried.' Again it is said: 'From the Ministers of all ranks down to the common people, it is not allowed to use gnld or silver.

"Should there be any cases of this decree being disregarded and these prohibitions infringed, the relations shall surely receive punishment.

"Again, there are many cases of persons who, having seen, say that they have not seen, or who, having not seen, say that they have seen, or who, having heard, say that they have not heard, or who, having not heard, say that they have beard, being deliberate liars, and devoid of truth in words and in sight.

"Again, there have been many cases in which slaves, both male and female, false to their masters in their poverty, betake themselves of their own accord to influential houses in quest of a livelihood, which influential houses forcibly detain and purchase them, and do not send them to their original owners.

"Again, there have been very many cases in which wives or concubines, when dismissed by their husbands, have after the lapse of years, married other husbands, as ordinary morality allows. Then their former husbands, after three or four years, have made greedy demands on the second husband's property, seeking their own gain.

"Again, there have been very many cases in which men, relying on their power, have rudely demanded people's daughters in marriage. In the interval, however, before going to his house, the girl has, of her own accord, married another, and the rude suitor has angrily made demands of the property of both families for his own gain.

"Again, there have been numerous cases of this kind. Sometimes a wife who has lost her husband marries another man after the lapse of ten or twenty years and becomes his spouse, or an unmarried girl is married for the first time. Upon this, people, out of envy of the married pair, have made them perform purgation.'"

"Again, there are cases in which women, who have become men's wives and who, being put away owing to their husbands' dislike of them, have, in their mortification at this injury, compelled themselves to become blemished slaves.

"Again, there are cases in which the husband, having frequent occasion to be jealous of his wife's illicit intercourse with others, voluntarily appeals to the authorities to decide the matter. Let such persons not lay their information until they have obtained, let us say, three credible witnesses to join with them in making a declaration. Why should they bring forward ill-considered plaints?

"Again, there have been cases of men employed on forced labor in border lands who, when the work was over and they were returning to their village, have fallen suddenly ill and lain down to die by the roadside. Upon this the inmates of the houses by the roadside say: 'Why should people be allowed to die on our road?' And they have accordingly detailed the companions of the deceased and compelled them to do purgation. For this reason it often happens that even if an elder brother lies down and dies on the road, the younger brother will refuse to take up his body for burial.

Again, there are cases of peasants being drowned in a river. The bystanders say: 'Why should we be made to have anything to do with drowned men?' They accordingly detain the drowned man's companions and compel them to do purgation. For this reason it often happens that even when an elder brother is drowned in a river his younger brother will not render assistance.

"Again, there are cases of people who, when employed on forced labor, cool, their rice by the roadside. Upon this the inmates of the houses by the roadside say: 'Why should people cook rice at their own pleasure on our road and have compelled them to do purgation'

"Again, there are cases when people have applied to others for the loan of pots in which to boil their rice, and the pots have knocked against something and have been upset. Upon this the owner of the pot compels purgation to be made.

"All such practises are habitual among the unenlightended vulgar. Let them now be discontinued without exception, and not be permitted again.

Again, there are cases in which peasants, when they are about to proceed to the capital, apprehensive lest their riding horses should be worn out and unable to go, give two fathoms of cloth and two bundles of hemp to men of the two provinces of Mikaha or Wohari, to hire them to feed their horses. After they have been to the capital and are on their way home, they make them a present of a spade, and then find that the men of Mikaha, etc., have not only failed to feed their horses properly, but have allowed them to die of starvation. In the case of horses of a superior class, they conceive covetous desires, and invent lying tales of their having been stolen, while in the case of mares which become pregnant in their house, they cause purgation to be made, and in the end make a plunder of the beast.

"Such things have come to our ears, We therefore now establish the following regulation:

"Whenever horses are left at livery or in any of the provinces along the highway, let the owner take with him the man whom he engages for this purpose, and make a full statement to the village elder, handing over to the latter at the same time the articles given as remuneration. It is unnecessary for him to make any further payment when be returns home. If be has caused the horse to suffer harm, he should get nothing.

"If any one disobeys this edict, a severe penalty shall be imposed.

"The dues payable to Market Commissioners, for main roads, and to ferrymen, are abolished, and lands are granted instead.

"Beginning with the Home provinces, and embracing the provinces in all four quarters, during the agricultural months," let every one apply himself early to the cultivation of the rice-land. It is not meet at such time to let them eat dainty food or drink sake. Let faithful messengers be appointed to intimate this to the Home provinces. And let the Kuni no Miyakko of the provinces in every quarter choose good messengers to urge the peasants to work in accordance with the edict."

Autumn, 8th month, 14th day. An edict was issued, saying:

"Going back to the origin of things, we find that it is Heaven and Earth with the male and female principles of nature, which guard the four seasons from mutual confusion. We find, moreover, that it is this Heaven and Earth which produces the ten thousand things. Amongst these ten thousand things Man is the most miraculously gifted. Among the most miraculously gifted beings, the sage takes the position of ruler. Therefore the Sage Rulers, viz., the Emperors, take Heaven as their exemplar in riding the World, and never for a moment dismiss from their breasts the thought of how men shall gain their fit place.

"Now as to the names of the early Princes, the Omi, Muraji, Tomo no Miyakko and Kuni no Miyakko have divided their various Be and allotted them severally to their various titles (or surnames). They afterward took the various Be of the people, and made them reside in the provinces and districts, one mixed up with another. The consequence has been to make father and child bear different surnames, and brothers to be reckoned of distinct families, while husbands and wives have names different from one another. One family is divided into five or split up into six, and both Court and country are therefore filled with contentious suits. No settlement has been come to, and the mutual confusion grows worse and worse. Let the various Be, therefore, beginning with those of the reigning Emperor and including those in the possession of the Omi, Muraji, etc., be, without exception, abolished, and let them become subjects of the State. Those who have become Tonio no Miyakko by borrowing the names of princes, and those who have become Omi or Muraji on the strength of the names of ancestors, may not fully apprehend our purport, and might think, if they heard this announcement without warning, that the names borrowed by their ancestors would become extinct. We therefore make this announcement beforehand, so that they may understand what are Our intentions.

"The children of rulers succeed one another in the government of the Empire, and it is well known that the names of the actual Emperor and of his Imperial ancestors will not be forgotten by the world. But the names of sovereigns are lightly given to rivers and plains, or common people are called by them. This is a truly fearful state of things. The appellations of sovereigns, like the sun and moon, will float afar: the names of those of the Imperial line will last forever, like unto Heaven and Earth. Such being our opinion, we announce as follows: 'Do ye all, from those of the Imperial line down to the Ministers, the Daibu, Omi, Muraji, and Tomo no Miyakko, who do Us service, in short all persons of whatever Uji (One book has 'royal subjects of whatever name'), give ear to what We say. with regard to the form of your service, We now abolish the former offices and constitute afresh the hundred bureaus. We shall, moreover, grant grades of rank and confer official dignities.

"Let the local Governors who are now being dispatched, and also the Kuni no Miyakko of the same provinces, give ear to what we say. In regard to the method of administration notified last year to the Court Assembly, let the previous arrangement be followed, and let the rice-lands which are received and measured be granted equally to the people, without distinction of persons. In granting rice-lands the peasants' houses should adjoin the land. Those whose houses lie near the lands must therefore have the preference. In this sense receive Our injunctions.

In regard to commuted taxes they should be collected from males only. "Laborers should be supplied at the rate of one for every fiftyhouses. The boundaries of the provinces should be examined and a description or map prepared, which should be brought here and produced for Our inspection. The names of the provinces and districts will be settled when you come.

"With respect to the places where embankments are to be constructed, or canals dug, and the extent of rice-land to be brought under cultivation, in the various provinces, uniform provision will be made for causing such work to be executed.

"Give ear to and understand these injunctions."

9th month. The Sbotoko Kuromaro, Takamuko no Hakase, was sent to Silla to cause them to send a hostage. Ultimately the tribute from Imna was discontinued.

In this month the Emperor occupied the temporary Palace of Kahadzu. (Some books have "detached Palace.")

In this year the rats of the province of Koshi drew together in troops by night and day, and took their departure toward the East.

(A.D. 647.) 3rd year, Spring, 1st month, 15th day. There was archery at the Court.

On this day Koryo and Silla sent messengers together to offer tribute.

Summer, 4th month, 29th day. An edict was issued as follows:

"The Empire was entrusted by the Sun-goddess to her descendants, with the words: 'My children, in their capacity of deities, shall rule it.'

(The phrase means to follow the way of the gods, or again to possess in oneself the way of the Gods.) For this reason, this country, since Heaven and Earth began, has been a monarchy. From the time that Our Imperial ancestor first ruled the land, there has been great concord in the Empire, and there has never been any factiousness. In recent times, however, the names, first of the gods, and then of the Emperors, have in some cases been separated (from their proper application) and converted into the Uji of Omi or Muraji. or they have been separated and made the qualifications of Miyakko, etc. In consequence of this, the minds of the people of the whole country take a strong partisan bias, and conceiving a deep sense of the me and thee, hold firmly each to their names. Moreover the feeble and incompetent Omi, Muraji, Tomo no Miyakko and Kuni no Miyakko make of such names their family names; and so the names of gods and the names of sovereigns are applied to persons and places in an unauthorized manner, in accordance with the bent of their own feelings. Now, by using the names of gods and the names of sovereigns as bribes, they draw to themselves the slaves of others, and so bring dishonor upon unspotted names. The consequence is that the minds of the people have become unsettled and the government of the country can not be carried on. The duty has therefore now devolved on Us in Our capacity as Celestial Divinity, to regulate and settle these things. In order to make them understood, and thereby to order the State and to order the people, We shall issue, one after another, a succession of edicts, one earlier, another later, one to-day and another tomorrow. But the people, -who have always trusted in the civilizing influence 104 exercised by the Emperors, and who are used to old customs, will certainly find it hard to wait until these edicts are made. We shall therefore remit to all, from Princes and Ministers down to the common people of all classes, the tax in lieu of service."

In this year Wogohori was pulled down and a Palace built.

The Emperor, having taken up his residence in the Palace of Wogohori, established a Law for Ceremonies, the regulations of which were as follows:

All persons holding official rank must draw up in lines to right and left outside the south gate at the hour of the Tiger, and wait there until the first appearance of the sun. They shall then enter the Court, and having made their obeisances, shall attend in the Hall. Those who come late will not be permitted to enter and take up their attendance. 'When the hour of the Horse arrives, they shall retire when they bear the sound of the bell. The officer whose business it is. to strike the bell shall wear a red apron. The bellstand shall be set up in the Middle Court,

The engineer of the rank of Daisen, Aratawi no Hirafu, Yamato Aya no Atahe, mistakenly dug a canal which he led to Naniha and thereby distressed the people. Upon this some one presented a memorial of remonstrance, and the Emperor made a decree, saying: "We unwisely gave ear to Hirafu's misrepresentations, and so dug this canal to no purpose. It is We who are to blame." That same day the work was discontinued.

Winter, 10th month, 11th day. The Emperor made a progress to the hot baths of Arima. He was accompanied by the Oho-omi of the Right and Left, and by the other Ministers and Daibu.

12th month, last day. The Emperor returned from the hot baths and stayed in the temporary Palace of Muko.

On this day the Palace of the Prince Imperial took fire, to the great marvel of the people of that time.

In this year there were instituted caps of seven kinds and thirteen grades.

The first was called Shoku-kwan. Of this there were two grades, the greater and the lesser. It was made of woven stuff, and embroidered on the borders. The color of the clothing was in both cases dark purple.

The second was called Shu-kwan. Of this there were two grades, the greater and the lesser. It was made of embroidered stuff. The border of the cap and the color of the clothing was the same as for the Shoku.-kwan.

The third was called Shi-kwan. Of this there were two grades, the greater and the lesser. It was made of purple material, with a border of woven stuff. The color of the clothing was light purple.

The fourth was called Kin-kwan. Of this there were two grades, the greater and the lesser. The greater Kin-kwan was made of Dai-haku-sen brocade, and had the cap-border of woven stuff: the lesser Kin-kwan was made of Sho-haku-sen brocade, and bad the cap-border of Dai-haku-sen brocade. The color of the clothing was in both cases true dark red.

The fifth was called Sei-kwan, and was made of blue silk. Of this there were two grades, the greater and the lesser. The greater Sei-kwan had a border of Dai-haku-sen brocade. The color of the clothing was in both cases deep violet.

The sixth was called Kok-kwan, and was made of black silk. Of this there were two grades, the greater and the lesser. The greater Kok-kwan had a border of wheel-pattern brocade. The lesser Kok-kwan had a border of diamondpattern brocade. The color of the clothing was in both cases green.

The seventh was called Kembu (the initial or lowest rank. It was also called Risshin). It was made of black silk and had a border of dark violet.

In addition to the above there were To-kwan, made of black silk. These caps had varnished gauze stretched behind.

Distinctions of rank were indicated by the border and the hair ornaments. The latter were in shape like a cicada. The hair ornaments of the grades from the Lesser Kin-kwan upward were of a combination of gold and silver: the hair ornaments of the Greater and Lesser Sei-kwan were made of silver: the hair ornaments of the Greater and Lesser Kokkwan were made of copper. The Kembu caps had no hair ornaments.

These caps were worn at Grand Assemblies, when foreign guests were entertained, and at the (Buddhist) maigre feasts of the fourth month and seventh month.

Silla sent Kim Chhyun-chhyu, a Superior Minister, of the rank of Greater Ason, and others to accompany the Hakase, Takamuko no Kuromaro, of Shotoko rank, and Oshikuma, Nakatomi no Muraji, of middle Shosen rank, and bring a present to the Emperor of a peacock and a parrot. Chhyunchhyu was made a hostage. He was a handsome man, who talked and smiled agreeably.

The Nutari barrier was constructed, and a barrier-settlement established. Old men talked to one another, saying: "The migration of the rats toward the East some years ago prefigured the making of this barrier."

(A.D. 648.) 4th year. Spring, 1st month, 1st day. The ceremony of New Year's congratulations took place.

In the evening the Emperor proceeded to the Palace of Toyosaki in Naniha.

2nd month, 1st day. Student priests were sent to Korea.

8th day. The Oho-omi Abe Invited the four classes to the Temple of Shitenoji, where, having brought in four images of Buddha, lie bad them enshrined within the pagoda. He constructed a figure of the wondrous Vulture Mountain, which he made by piling up drums on one another.

Summer, 4th month, 1st day. The old caps were discontinued. The Oho-omi of the Left and Right, however, continued to wear the old caps.

This year Silla sent envoys bearing tribute.

The barrier of Ihabune was put to rights as a precaution against the Yemisbi. Eventually subjects from the provinces of Koshi and Shinano were selected, and a barrier-settlement for the first time established.

5th year. Spring, 1st month, 1st day. The New Year's congratulations took place.

2nd month. Nineteen cap grades were instituted, as follows:

First	Dai-shiki	(greater woven-stuff)
Second	Sbc-shiki	(lesser woven-stuff)
Third	Dai-shu	(greater embroidery)
Fourth	Sho-shu,	(lesser embroidery)
Fifth	Dai-shi	(greater purple)
Sixth	Sho-shi	(lesser purple)
Seventh	Upper Dai-kwa	(greater flower)
Eighth.	Lower Dai-kwa	(greater flower)
Ninth	Upper Sho-kwa	(Iesser flower)
Tenth	Lower Sho-kwa	(lesser flower)
Eleventh	Upper Dai-sen	(greater mountain)
Twelfth	Lower Dai-sen	(greater mountain)
Thirteenth	Upper Sho-en	(lesser mountain)
Fourteenth	Lower Sho-sen	(lesser mountain)
Fifteenth	Upper Dai-otsu	
Sixteenth	Lower Dai-otsu	
Seventeenth	Upper Sho-otsu	
Eighteenth	Lower Sbo-otsu	
Nineteenth	Risshin	(Promotion or advancement)

In this month an order was given to the Hakase, Takamuko no Kuromaro, and the Buddhist Priest Bin to establish Eight Departments of State and one hundred bureaus.

3rd month, 17th day. Abe no Oho-omi died. The Emperor proceeded to the Shujaku gate, where be raised up lamentations for him and showed much emotion. The Empress Dowager, the Prince Imperial, and the other Princes, together with the Ministers of every rank, all, following his example, mourned and lamented.

24th day. Hiuga, Soga no Omi (styled Musashi) slandered the Oho-omi Kurayamada to the Prince Imperial, saying: "Maro, thy servant's elder brother by a different mother, is watching the opportunity of the Prince Imperial making an excursion to the seaside, in order to do him a mischief. He will ere long commit treason." The Prince Imperial believed this. The Emperor sent Ohotomo no Komano Muraji, Alikuni no Maro no Kimi, and Hodzumi no Kurafu no Omi to the Obo-omi, Kurayamada no Maro, and questioned him as to the truth of the charge of treason. The Oho-omi answered and said: "I will have a personal interview with the Emperor, and shall then answer to the charge brought against me." The Emperor again sent Mikuni no Maro no Kimi and Hodzumi, Kurafu no Omi, to investigate the circumstances of the treason. The Oho-omi, Maro, again answered as before. The Emperor was therefore about to raise an armed force and surround therewith the Oho-onii's house, when the Oho-omi, taking with him his two sons, Hoshi and Akagoma (also called Mawosu), fled by way of Chinu toward the boundary of the province of Yamato. Before this, Koshi, the Oho-omi's eldest son, was already staying in Yamato, where he was building the Temple.

(This means that he was staying in the Yamada house.) Now being suddenly apprised that his father was coming thither in flight, he went out to meet him at the great Tsuki tree in Imaki. Having approached, he took the lead and entered the Temple. Then he looked back to the Oho-omi and said: "Koshi desires to advance straight on in person, and oppose the army which is coming." But the Oho-omi would not allow it. That night Koshi conceived the idea of burning the Palace (the Palace of Woharida is meant), and went on assembling troops.

25th day. The Oho-omi addressed his eldest son Koshi, saying: "Dost thou love thy life?" Koshi answered and said: "I love it not." The Oho-omi thereupon harangued the priests of the Yamada Temple, his eldest son Koshi and some tens of other persons, saying: "Shall one who is in the position of vassal contrive treason against his Lord? Shall the duty of a son to a father be brought to nothing? This temple was originally built, not for me personally, but under a vow for the sake of the Emperor. I have now been slandered by Musashi, and I fear that I shall be unjustly put to death. With so near a prospect of the yellow springs, I would withdraw from life still cherishing fidelity in my bosom, and the object of my coming to this Temple is that my last moments may be made easier."

When a one speaking, he opened the door of the Buddha Hall and uttered a vow, saying: "In all future births and existences, let me not have resentment against my sovereign!" When he had made this vow, he strangled himself and died. His wife and children, to the number of eight persons, sacrificed themselves with him.

On this day, Oho-tomo no Koma no Muraji and Soga no Iliuga no Omi were sent as Generals in command of a body of troops to pursue the Oho-omi. General Ohotomo no Muraji and his colleague bad gone as far as Kuroyama when Mu, Hashi no Muraji, and Omimaro, Uneme no Omi, came running from the Yamada Temple, and brought information that the Obo-omi Soga, with his three sons and one daughter, had already committed suicide together by strangulation. The Generals therefore returned from Tajihi no Saka.

26th day. The wife, children, and personal attendants of the Oho-omi Yamada, who committed suicide by strangulation, were many. Kurafu, Hodzumi no Omi, arrested in a body the Oho-omi's people, viz.: Tsukushi, Taguchi no Omi, and others, placed cangues round their necks, and tied their hands behind their backs. That night, Maro, Ki no Omi, Hiuga, Soga no Omi, and Kurafu, Hodzumi no Omi, having surrounded the Temple with an armed force, called Shiho, Mononobe no Futauta no Miyakko, and ordered him to cut off the Obo-omi's head. Upon this Futsuta no Shiho drew his sword, raised up the body on its point, yelled and reviled, and then cut it off.

30th day. There were executed, as implicated with the Oho-omi, Soga no Yamada, Tsukushi, Taguchi no Omi, Miminashi no Dōtoko, Takada no Sikowo Nukadabe no Yumasu no Muraji, Hada no Adera and others, fourteen persons in all. Nine were strangled, and fifteen banished.

In this month, messengers were sent to take over the property of the Oho-omi, Yamada. Among his property was a beautiful book with the inscription, "Book belonging to the Prince Imperial," and a valuable object inscribed "Property of the Prince Imperial." When the messengers returned and reported the circumstances of their having taken over the property, the Prince Imperial recognized for the first time that the heart of the Oho-omi had remained pure and unspotted. He was seized with shame and remorse for the past, and bewailed his fate incessantly. Hiuga no Orai was accordingly appointed Viceroy of Tsukushi. The people of the time said to one another, "Is not this a disguised banishment?"

When Sogo no Miyakko hime, consort of the Prince Imperial, heard that her father the Obo-omi had been decapitated by Shiho, she took it deeply to heart and grieved bitterly. She detested hearing Shiho's name mentioned, and so her personal attendants, whenever they had occasion to speak of salt (shiho), altered the word and called it Kitashi. At last Miyakko hime died of a broken heart. When the Prince Imperial heard that she had passed away, he was grieved and deeply shocked, and bewailed her loss exceedingly. Upon this Mitsu, Nunaka Kahara no Fubito, came forward and presented verses of poety as follows:

> On a mountain stream
> Two mandarin-ducks there be,
> Well matched together:
> But the wife who was a like mate for me
> Who is it that has taken away?

This was the first verse.

> Though on every tree
> The flowers are blooming,
> How can it be that
> My darling wife
> Does not blossom again?

This was the second verse.

The Prince Imperial, with a sigh of deep despair, praised the verses, saying: "How beautiful! how pathetic! "So he gave him his lute and made him sing them. He also presented him with four hiki of silk, twenty tan of cloth, and two bags of floss silk.

Summer, 4th month, 20th day. Kose no Tokodako no Omi, of the Shoshi rank, was granted the rank of Daishi, and was made Oho-omi of the Left.

Ohotomo no 'Nagatoko no Muraji (styled Numakahi) of Shashi rank, was granted the rank of Daishi, and was made Obo-omi of the Right.

5th month, 1st day. Shikofu, Miwa no Kimi, of Lower Sh6kwa rank, Tsunomaro, Harahibe, no Muraji 137 of Upper Daisen rank, and others were sent to Silla.

This year, the Queen of Silla sent Kim Ta-sya, Sa-son of Sa-tok-pu, as hostage. He had a suite of thirty persons: One Buddhist priest, two Si-rang, one Assistant, one Usher, five Chung-kek, ten Artists, one Interpreter, and sixteen servants of various kinds - in all thirty-seven persons.

(A.D. 650.) Hakuchi,111 1st year, Spring, 1st month, 1st day. The Imperial chariot proceeded to the Palace of Ajifu, where the Emperor viewed the ceremonies of the New Year's congratulations.

On this day the Imperial chariot returned to the Palace.

2nd month, 9th day. Shikofu, Kusakabe no Muraji, Governor of the Province of Anato, presented to the Emperor a white pheasant, saying: "Nihe, a relation of Obito, the Kuni no Miyakko, caught it on the 9th day of the first month on Mount Wonoyama." Upon this inquiry was made of the Lords of Pokcho, who said: "In the eleventh year of Yung-p'ing in the reign of Ming Ti of the Later Han Dynasty, white pheasants were seen in a certain place." Further inquiry was made of the Buddhist priests, who answered and said: "With our ears we have not heard, nor with our eyes have we seen such. May it please Your Majesty to order a general amnesty; and so give joy to the hearts of the people."

The Priest Doto said: "At one time Korye desired to build a Buddhist temple. There was no place which was not examined for this purpose. Then in a certain place a white deer was seen quietly moving, and eventually a temple was built on this spot. It was called the Temple of the Park of the White Deer, and the practise of the Buddhist Law was there permanently established. Again, a white sparrow was seen at the farmstead of a certain temple. The people of the country all said that it was a good omen. Moreover, envoys sent to Great Thang brought back a dead crow with three legs. The people of the country again said that this was a good omen. Though these things are trifles, yet they are deemed of favorable omen. Much more is this so in the case of a white pheasant."

The Priest Bin said: "This is to be deemed a lucky omen, and it may reasonably be accounted a rare object. I have respectfully heard that when a Ruler extends his influence to all four quarters, then will white pheasants be seen. They appear, moreover, when a Ruler's sacrifices are not in mutual disaccord, and when his banquets and costumes are in due measure. Again, when a Ruler is of frugal habits, white pheasants are made to come forth on the hills. Again, they appear when the Ruler is sage and humane. In the time of the Emperor Ch'eng Wang of the Chou Dynasty, the Yueh-shang family brought and presented to the Emperor a white pheasant, saying: 'We were told by the old men of our country: "What a long time it has been since there have been any exceptional storms or long-continued rains, and that the great rivers and the sea have not surged up over the land! Three years have now elapsed. We think that in the Central Land there is a Sage. Would it not be well to go and pay your respects at his Court?" We have therefore come, having tripled our interpreters.' Again, in the first year of Hien-ning in the reign of Wu-ti of the Tsin Dynasty, one was seen in the Sung-tsze. This is accordingly a favorable omen. A general amnesty ought to be granted."

Upon this the white pheasant was let loose in the garden.

15th day. The array of guards at Court was like that on the occasion of a New Year's reception. The Oho-omi of the Right and Left and all the functionaries formed four lines outside of the purple gate. Ihimushi, Ahata no Omi, and three others were made to take the pheasant's litter and move off ahead, while the Oho-omi of the Right and Left at the head of all the functionaries, and Phung-chyang, Lord of Pekche, his younger brother Se-syong, Chhyung-seung, the physician to the King of Koryo, by name Mo-chhi, the scholar attached to the Court of Silla, and others, advanced into the Central Court. These four men, viz., Maro, Mikuni no Kimi, Takami, Wina no Kimi, Mikaho, Miwa no Kimi, and Maro Kida, Ki no Omi, taking up the pheasant's litter in turn, advanced in front of the Hall. Then the Oho-oini of the Right and Left approached and held the litter by the forward end. The Prince of Ise, Maro, Alikuni no Kimi, and Woguso, Kura no Omi, took hold of the hinder end of the litter and placed it before the Imperial throne. The Emperor straightway called the Prince Imperial, and they took it and examined it together. The Prince Imperial having retired, made repeated obeisances, and caused the Oho-omi Kose to offer a congratulatory address, saying: "The Ministers and functionaries offer their congratulations. Inasmuch as Your Majesty governs the Empire with serene virtue, there is here a white pheasant, produced in the western region. This is a sign that Your Majesty will continue for a thousand autumns and ten thousand years peacefully to govern the Greater-eight-islands of the four quarters. it is the prayer of the Ministers, functionaries, and people that they may serve Your Majesty with the utmost zeal and fidelity."

Having finished this congratulatory speech, he made repeated obeisances. The Emperor said:

"When a sage Ruler appears in the world and rules the Empire, Heaven is responsive to him, and manifests favorable omens. In ancient times, during the reign of Cheng-wang of the Chou Dynasty, a ruler of the Western land, and again in the time of Ming Ti of the Han Dynasty, white pheasants were seen. In this our Land of Japan, during the reign of the Emperor Homuda,'" a white crow made its nest in the Palace. In the time of the Emperor Oho-sazaki, a Dragon-horse appeared in the West."' This shows that from ancient times until now, there have been many cases of auspicious omens appearing in response to virtuous rulers. What we call phoenixes, unicorns, white pheasants, white crows, and such like birds and beasts, even including herbs and trees, in short all things having the property of significant response, are favorable omens and auspicious signs produced by Heaven and Earth. Now that wise and enlightened sovereigns should obtain such auspicious omens is meet and proper. But why should We, who are so empty and shallow, have this good fortune? It is no doubt wholly due to our Assistants, the Ministers, Omi, Muraji, Tomo no Miyakko and Kuni no Miyakko, each of whom, with the utmost loyalty, conforms to the regulations that are made. For this reason, let all, from the Ministers down to the functionaries 'with pure hearts reverence the gods of Heaven and Earth, and one and all accepting the glad omen, make the Empire to flourish."

Again be commanded, saying:

"The provinces and districts in the four quarters having been placed in our charge by Heaven, We exercise supreme rule over the Empire. - Now in the province of Anato, ruled over by Our divine ancestors, this auspicious omen has appeared. For this reason We proclaim a general amnesty throughout the Empire, and begin a new year-period, to be called Haku-chi. Moreover we prohibit the flying of falcons within the limits of the province of Anato."

Presents were made to the Ministers, Daibu and officials of lower rank down to the clerks, varying in value according to their rank. Hereupon the local Governor, Shikofu, Kusa-kabe no Muraji, was commended and granted the rank of Daiseni together with liberal presents. The commuted taxes and corvies of Anato were remitted for three years.

Summer, 4th month. Silla sent Envoys to offer tribute.

One book says: "In the reign of this Emperor the three countries of Koryo, Pekche and Silla sent envoys bearing tribute every year."

Winter, 10th month. In respect of the tombs which had been demolished in order to include the ground in a site for a Palace, and of the people who had been made to remove for the same purpose, presents were given, varying in value. This having been done, the chief builder, Hirafu Aratawi no Atabe, was sent to set up the boundary-posts of the Palace.

In this month the construction was begun of an embroidery figure of Buddha sixteen feet in height with its attendant Bosatsu, and of figures of beings of the eight classes - forty-six figures in all.

In this year, Ohoguchi, Aya no Yamaguchi no Atahe, in obedience to an Imperial order, carved one thousand images of Buddha.

(A.D. 651.) Winter, 12th month, last day. More than 2100 priests and nuns were invited to the Palace of Ajifu, and made to read the Issaikyo.

That night over 2700 lights were lit in the courtyard of the Palace, and there were caused to be read the Antaku and Dosoku Sutras, etc. Upon this, the Emperor removed his residence from Oho-gohori to the new Palace. It received the name of the Palace of Naniha no Nagara no Toyosaki.

This year the Silla tribute-envoys, Chi-man, of Sa-son rank, and his companions anchored at Tsukushi, wearing garments of the Thang country. The Government, disgusted at this wanton change of habit, reproved them and drove them back again. At this time Kose no Oho-omi addressed the Emperor, saying: "If we do not give a blow to Silla at this present time, we shall certainly have to regret it afterward. Now as to the manner of giving a blow to Silla, we can do so without raising a sword. From the port of Naniha as far as Tsukushi let the surface of the sea be covered with ships, one touching another. Then if Silla be summoned and called to an account for her offenses, it will be easy for us to gain our object."

(A.D. 652.) 3rd year, Spring, 1st month, 1st day. When the New Year's ceremonies were over, the Imperial chariot proceeded to the Palace of Oho-gohori.

20th day. The explanations of the Sutras were discontinued. From this day forward rain began to fall continually, lasting for nine days. It demolished buildings, and destroyed the young rice-plants in the fields. Many men, horses, and oxen were drowned.

In this month the registers of population were prepared. Fifty houses were made a township, and for each township there was appointed an elder. The senior member of the family was always made the head of the household. The houses were all associated in groups of five for mutual protection, with one elder to supervise them one with another.

Autumn, 9th month. The building of the Palace was completed. It is impossible adequately to describe the appearance of the Palace Halls.

Winter, 12th month, last day. The priests and nuns of the Empire were invited to the interior of the Palace and entertained with meager fare. Plentiful alms were given, and lights kindled.

(A.D. 653.) Autumn, 7th month. Takada no Nemaro and his colleagues, the Ambassadors sent to Great Thang, were drowned by the sinking of their ship in the Gate 1160 of Takashima, off the coast of Satsuma. Only five men, who lashed themselves to a plank, floated ashore on the island of Takashima. They knew not what to do, until one of the five, named Kadobe no Kogane, gathered bamboos and made of them a raft, with which they anchored at the island of Shitoji-shima These five men passed six days and six nights without any food whatever. Thereupon Kogane was complimented by the Emperor, advanced in rank, and presents given him.

This year the Prince Imperial petitioned the Emperor, saying: "I wish the Imperial residence were removed to the Yamato capital." The Emperor refused to grant his request. Upon this the Prince Imperial took with him the Empress Dowager, the Empress Hashibito, and the younger Imperial Princes, and went to live in the temporary Palace of Asuka no Kahabe in Yamato. At this time the Ministers and Daibu, with the various functionaries, all followed and changed their residence. The Emperor resented this, and wished to cast away the national Dignity. He bad a palace built in Yamazaki and sent a song to th~ Empress Hashibito, saying:

> "The pony which I keep,
> I put shackles on
> And led it not out:
> Can any one have seen
> The pony which I keep?"

5tb year, Spring, 1st month, 1st day. In the night the rats migrated toward the Yamato capitai.

Winter, 10th month, 1st day. The Prince Imperial, being informed that the Emperor bad taken ill, proceeded to the Naniha Palace with the Empress Dowager, the Empress Hashibito, and also accompanied by the younger Imperial Princes and Ministers.

10th day. The Emperor died in the State Bedchamber. He was temporarily interred in the southern courtyard. Dotoko, Mozu no Hashi no Muraji, of Upper Shosen rank, superintended the business of the Palace of Temporary Interment.

12th month, 8th day. He was buried in the misasagi of Shinaga at Ohosaka.

On this day, the Prince Imperial, accompanied by the Empress Dowager, changed his residence to the Temporary Palace of Kahabe in Yamato. Old people said: "The migration of the rats to the Yamato capital was an omen of the transference of the capital thither."

In this year, Koryo, Pekche and Silla sent ambassadors of condolence.

THE LATER RULERS

BOOK XXVI

THE EMPRESS AME-TOYO-TAKARA IKASHI-HI TARASHI-HIME

The Empress Ame-toyo-takara ikashi-hi tarashi-hime [later known as Saimei Tenno] first married the Emperor Tachibana no toyohi's grandson, Prince Takamuku, and bore to him the Imperial Prince Aya. She was afterward married to the Emperor Oki-naga tarashi hi hiro-nuka, to whom she bore two sons and one daughter. In his second year she was raised to the rank of Empress-consort, as may be seen in the history of the Emperor Oki-naga tarashi-hi hiro-nuka. In the thirteenth year of his reign, Winter, the tenth month, the Emperor Oki-naga tarashi-hi hiro-nuka died. In the first mouth of the following year the Empress assumed the Imperial Dignity. In the sixth month of the fourth year of the new reign, she resigned the Dignity to the Emperor Ame-yorodzu-toyohi, and was entitled Empress Dowager. The Emperor Ame-yorodzu-toyohi died in the tenth month of the later fifth Year.

(A.D. 655.) 1st year, Spring, 1st month, 3rd day. The Empress Dowager assumed the Imperial Dignity in the Palace of Asuka no Itabuki.

Summer, 5th month, ist day. In the midst of the Void there was seen one riding on a dragon, who resembled a man of Thang in appearance. He bad on a broad bat of green oiled stuff. He rode fast from the peak

75

of Katsuraki and disappeared on Mount Ikoma. When it became noon, he galloped off over the firs of Sumiyoshi in a westerly direction.

Winter, 10th month, 13th day. There was a Palace in course of construction at Woharida which it was intended to roof with tiles. But in the recesses of the mountains and on the broad valleys, much of the timber with which it was proposed to erect the Palace buildings rotted. In the end the work was put a stop to, and no building was erected.

This winter the Palace of Asuka no Itabuki was burned, and the Empress therefore removed her residence to the Palace of Asuka no Kahara.

(A.D. 656.) In this year a fresh site for a Palace was fixed upon at Asuka no Wokamoto.

At this time, Koryo, Pekche and Silla together sent envoys to offer tribute. Dark purple curtains were drawn round this Palace site for them, and they were entertained there. At last the Palace buildings were erected, and the Empress removed into them. This Palace was called the later Palace of Asuka no Wokamoto.

Tamu Peak was crowned with a circular enclosure. Moreover on the summit of the Peak, close by where two tsuki trees grew, a lofty building was erected to which the name was given of the Palace of Futa-tsuki. It was also called Amatsu miya.

At this time public works were in favor. Navvies were employed to dig a canal from the western end of Mount Kagu yama as far as the Mountain of Iso no kami. Two hundred barges were loaded with stones from the Iso no Kami Mountain and hauled with the current to the mountain on the east of the Palace, where the stones were piled up to form a wall. The people of that day reviled the work, saying: "This mad canal, which has wasted the labor of over 30,000 men! This wall-building, which has wasted the labor of over 70,000 men! And the timber for the Palace which has rotted! And the top of the mountain which has collapsed!"

Again they reviled, saying: "May the mound built at Iso no kami break down of itself as fast as it is built!"

(A.D. 658.) Summer, 4th mouth. Abe no Omi went on an expedition against the Yemishi in command of a fleet of 180 ships. The Yemishi of the two districts of Aita and Nushiro were struck with fear, and tendered their submission. Hereupon the ships were drawn up in order of battle in the bay of Aita. A Yemishi of Aita named Omuka came forward and made an oath, saying: "It is not by reason of the arrival of the Imperial forces that we slaves carry bows and arrows, but because it is our nature to live upon animal food. If we have provided bows and arrows against the Imperial forces, may the Gods of the bay of Aita take note of it! We will serve the Government with pure hearts."

Omuka was accordingly granted the rank of Upper Shaotsu, and local governors were established in the two districts of Nushiro and Tsugaru. Ultimately the Yemishi of Watari no Shima were summoned together at the shore of Arima and a great feast provided them, after which they were dismissed home.

5th month. A grandson of the Empress named Prince Takeru died. He was eight years of age. His remains were deposited in a temporary tomb which was raised for him over the Imaki valley. The Empress had always esteemed her grandson highly for his obedient conduct. She was therefore beside herself with grief, and her emotion was exceeding great. Sending for the Ministers, she said:

"After ten thousand years and a thousand autumns he must be interred along with us in our own misasagi.

So she made songs, saying:

> On the Hill of Womure
> In Imaki—
> If but a cloud

Arose, plain to be seen,
Why should lament?

This was the first song.

"I never thought
That he was young
As the young grass
By the riverside whither one tracks
The deer wounded by an arrow."

This was the second song.

Like the flowing water
Of the River Asuka.
Which surges as it flows,
Unceasingly
I long for him!

This was the third song.

The Empress sang these songs from time to time, and lamented bitterly.

In this month, the Buddhist priests Chitsu and Chitatsu went by, the Empress's command to Great Thang on board a Silla ship, where they received instruction from the teacher of religion," Hsuan-ts'ang, on the philosophy of things without life and living beings.

Winter, 10th month, 15th day. The Empress visited the hot baths of Ki. The Empress, remembering her Imperial grandson, Prince Takeru, grieved and lamented. She exclaimed) saying:

Though I pass over the mountains
And cross the seas
Yet can I never forget
The pleasant Region of Imaki.

The first

With the harbor's
Ebbing tide,
An the sea goes down,
With the darkness behind me
Leaving him, I must go -
The dear one.
My young child!
Leaving him, I must go.

The second.

She commanded Mari, Hada no Oho-kura no Miyakko, saying: "Let these verses be handed down and let them not be forgotten by the world."

11th month, 3rd day. Soga no Akaye no Omi, the official who had charge during the Empress's absence, addressed the Imperial Prince Arima, saying: "There are three faults in the Empress's administration of the affairs of Government. The first is that she builds treasuries on a great scale, wherein she collects the riches of the people. The second is that she wastes the public grain revenue in digging long canals. The third is that she loads barges with stones and transports them to be piled up into a hill." The Imperial Prince Arima, recognizing Akaye's friendly disposition toward himself, was gratified, and replied, saying: "I have only now come to an age when I am fit to bear arms."

5th day. The Imperial Prince Arima proceeded to the house of Akaye, where he went up into an upper story and conspired with him. A legrest broke of itself. They both recognized that this was a bad omen, and swore to one another to proceed no further. The Imperial Prince returned home, where he was staying for the night, when at midnight Akaye sent Shibi, Mononobe no Yenowi no Muraji, in command of the laborers engaged in building the Palace, to surround the Imperial Prince Arima in his house at Ichifu, and straightway dispatched a mounted courier to inform the Empress.

9th day. The Imperial Prince Arima, with Oho-ishi, Mori no Kimi, Kusuri, Sakahibe no Muraji, and Konoshiro, Shihoya no Muraji, were arrested, and sent to the hot springs of Ki. His toneri Yonemaro, Nihitabe no Muraji, followed him.

Thereupon the Prince Imperial in person questioned the Imperial Prince Arima, saying: "Why didst thou plot treason?" He answered and said: "Heaven and Akaye know. I do not at all understand."

11th day. Kuniso, Tajihi no Wosaha no Muraji, was sent to strangle the Imperial Prince Arima at the Fujishiro acclivity. On this day Konoshiro, Shihoya no Muraji, nd the toneri Yonemaro, Nihitabe no Muraji, were executed at the Fujishiro, acclivity. When Konosbiro, Shihoya no Muraji, was about to be executed he said: "I request that my right hand may be made a national treasure." Oho-ishi, Mori no Kimi, was banished to the province of Kamitsukenu, and Kusuri, Sakahibe no Muraji, to the province of Wohari.

One book says: "The Imperial Prince Arima, with Akaye, So-a no Omi, Konosbiro, Shiboya no Muraji, Oho-isbi, Mori no Kimi, and Kusuri, Sakahibe no Muraji, divined the future of their treasonous conspiracy by drawing slips of paper." One book says: "The Imperial Prince Arima said: 'First of all we will burn the Palace. Then with five hundred men for a day and two nights we will waylay the Empress at the harbor of Muro, and speedily with a fleet cutting off the land of Ahaji, make as it were a prison. This can be easily accomplished.' Some one objected, saying: 'It can not be so. For all your plans, the faculty of carrying them out is wanting. At the present time, Your Imperial Highness is only nineteen years of age, and has not yet attained to manhood. You must first reach manhood and then you will gain the faculty.'" Another book says: "When the Imperial Prince Arima was plotting treason along with a judicial officer, the leg of the Imperial Prince's arm-rest broke of itself without cause, but he did not cease from conspiring, and was eventually executed."

In this year, Hirafu, Abe no Hikida no Omi, Warden of the land of Koshi, went on an expedition against the Sushen. He presented to the Emperor two live white bears.

The Buddhist priest Chiyu made a south-pointing chariot.

It was reported from the province of Idzumo: "On the shore of the northern sea the fish are dying in heaps three feet in depth. In size they resemble the globe-fish. They have the beaks of sparrows and thorny scales several inches long. The common people say that they are sparrows which have gone into the sea and become changed into fish, and give them the name of 'sparrow-fish.'"

One book says: "In the seventh month of the sixth year, Pekche sent envoys with the following message to the Enipress: 'Great Thang and Silla have joined their powers for an attack upon us. They have taken away as prisoners King Wicha, his Queen 'and the Heir to the Throne. Our Government has therefore stationed troops on the northwestern frontier and repaired the fortifications as an indication that the mountains and rivers are blocked."

Moreover Tsuratari, Adzumi no Muraji, of Lower Shokwa rank, who bad gone as Envoy to the Western Seal returned from Pekche and reported that Pekche had returned after a successful expedition against Silla. At this time a horse of his own accord went round the Golden Hall of a temple night and day without ceasing, and only stopping to graze.

One book says: "This was an echo of its destruction by the enemy in the year Kanoye Saru."

(A.D. 659.) A fox bit off the end of a creeper which a laborer of the district of Ou held in his band, and went off with it. Moreover, a dog brought in his mouth a dead man's hand and forearm and laid it in the Ifuya shrine. (Signs that the Empress was about to die.)

Again, the Koryo envoys had a bear-skin, on which they put a price of sixty pounds of floss silk. The market commissioner laughed and went away.

A Koryo painter, named Komaro, on the day on which he entertained guests of his own surname in his private house, borrowed seventy official polar-bear skins for them to sit upon. The guests were ashamed and astonished and went away.

(A.D. 660.) 6th year, Spring, 1st month, 1st day. The Koryo envoys, the Eul-syang, Ha Chhyu-mun, and his suite, numbering over one hundred persons, anchored in Tsukushi.

3rd month. Abe no Omi was sent on an expedition with a fleet of 200 ships against the land of Su-shen. Abe no Omi made some Yemishi of Nlichinoku embark on board his own ship. They arrived close to a great river. Upon this over a thousand Yemishi of Watari-shima assembled on the seashore and made a camp facing the river. Two men of this camp came forward and called out hurriedly, saying: "The Su-shen fleet has arrived in great force and threatens to slay us. We pray, therefore, to be allowed to cross the river and to serve the Government. Abe no Omi sent a boat to go and fetch these two Yemishi, and inquired from them where the enemy were concealed and the number of their ships. The two Yemishi accordingly pointed out the place of their concealment, saying: "There are over twenty ships." Thereupon he sent messengers to summon them, but they refused to come. Abe no Omi accordingly heaped upon the beach colored silk stuffs, weapons, iron, etc., to excite their cupidity. The Su-shen people thereupon drew up their fleet in order, and tying feathers to poles, raised them aloft by way of flags. They approached with equal oars and came to a pause in a shallow place. Then from one of the ships they sent forth two old men who went round the colored silk stuffs and other articles which bad been piled up, examining them closely. They then changed the single garments they had on, and each taking up one piece of cloth in his band, went on board their ship and departed. Presently the old men came back again, took off the exchanged garments, and laying them down along with the cloth they bad taken away, went on board their ship and departed. Abe no Omi sent several ships to fetch them, but they refused to come, and returned to the island of Herobe. (Herobe is a separate part of Watarishima.) After some time they asked for peace, but Abe no Omi refused altogether to listen to them. So they betook themselves to their own palisades and fought. At this time Mamukatsu, Noto no Omi, was slain by the enemy. While the battle was still going on, and was not yet fought out, the enemy, finding that they were being beaten, put to death their own wives and children.

Summer, 5th month, 8th day. The Koryo Envoy, the Eul-syang, Ha Chhyu-mun, and his suite arrived at the official residence of Naniha.

In this month, the officials, by order of the Empress, prepared one hundred raised seats "and one hundred Nokesa, and held a Ninwo Hanya meeting.

Moreover, the Prince Imperial for the first time made a clepsydra, by which he caused the people to know the hours.

Again, Abe no Hikida no Omi presented to the Empress more than fifty savages.

Again, a Mount Sumi was built near the pond of Iso no Kami, as high as a pagoda. On this occasion forty-seven men of Su-shen were entertained.

Again, the people of the whole country carried arms without reason when passing to and fro on the highways. The old people of the country said: "This perhaps denotes the destruction of the Land of Pekche."

(A.D. 661.) 7th year, Spring, 1st month, 6th day. The Imperial ship first put to sea for the expedition against the West.

3rd mouth, 25th day. The Imperial ship returned to Una no Ohotsu, where the Empress occupied the temporary Palace of Ihase, the name of which the Empress altered to Nagatsu.

At this time trees belonging to the Shrine of Asakura were cut down and cleared away in order to build this Palace. Therefore the gods were angry and demolished the building. Some were also struck, and in consequence the Grand Treasurer and many of those in waiting took ill and died.

23rd day. Tamna, for the first time, sent Prince A-pha-ki and others with tribute.

In the writing of Hakatoko, Yuki no Muraji, it is stated:

On the 25th day of the Ist month of the year Kanoto Tori (A.D. 661), we arrived at Yueh-chow on our return journey. On the 1st day of the 4th month, leaving Yueh-chow, we proceeded homeward in an easterly direction, and on the 7th arrived south of Mount Ch'eng-an-shan. On the 8th day at cock-crow we put out to sea with a southwest wind in our favor, but in mid-ocean we lost our way and tossed about, undergoing much suffering. On the 9th day at nightfall we reached the island of Tamna with great difficulty. There we induced Prince A-pha-ki and eight other natives of the island to embark with us in the guest-ship to the end that we might present them to the Imperial Court. On the 23rd day of the 25th month, we presented them to the Imperial Court at Asakura. This was the first time that Tamna was received at Court. Moreover, the envoys, who had been slandered by Tarushima, Yamato no Aya no Atahe, a follower of Chihung, received no gracious command. These envoys were wroth, and their anger penetrated to the gods of High Heaven, who with a thunderbolt killed Tarushima." The men of that day said of this: "The divine vengeance of Yamato is near."

6th month. Prince Ise died.

Autumn, 7th month, 24th day. The Empress died in the Palace of Asakura.

8th month, 1st day. The Prince Imperial, in attendance on the Empress's remains, returned as far as the Palace of Ihase. That evening, on the top of Mount Asakura, there was a demon wearing a great hat, who looked down on the funeral proceedings. All the people uttered exclamations of wonder.

Winter, 10th month, 7th day. The Empress's funeral train returning, put to sea. Hereupon the Prince Imperial, having come to an anchor in the same place, was filled with grief and longing for the Empress. So he sung to himself, saying:

"Longing as I do
For a sight of thee,
Now that I have arrived here, Even thus do I long
Desirous of a sight of thee!"

[The later passages become, more and more, mere chronicles of commonplace events and entertainments, with an occasional plot or revolt. The closing pages of the thirtieth and last book, which follow, are typical of the rest.]

(A.D. 697.) 11th year, Spring, 1st month, 7th day. An entertainment was given to the Ministers and Daibu.

11th day. Presents of rice in ear of various values were given to all widowers, widows, orphans, and childless persons, to those suffering from grave disease, and to those who from poverty were unable to support themselves, throughout the Empire.

16th day. An entertainment was given to the Ministers and public functionaries.

2nd month, 28th day. Kunimi, Tahema no Mlabito, of Jiki-kw6-ichi rank, was appointed Grand Tutor of the Heir Apparent, Atomi, Michi no Mabito, of Jiki-kwo-san rank, was appointed Director of the Spring

Palace, and Ahamochi, Kose no Ason, of Jiki-dai-shi rank, Assistant Director.

3rd month, 8th day. A public great-congregation was held at the Eastern Palace.

Summer, 4th month, 4tb day. Ranks, from that of Jo to that of Jiki, were conferred on the selected persons for office, discrimination being made in the case of each.

7th day. The Empress Jito went to the Palace of Yoshino.

14th day. Envoys were sent to pray to Hirose and Tatsuta.

On this day the Empress arrived from Yoshino.

5th month, 8th day. Daibu were sent as envoys to the various shrines to pray for rain.

6th month, 2nd day. Criminals were pardoned.

6th day. An Imperial order was made that Sutras should be read in the temples of the Home provinces.

15th day. Persons of the fifth and lower ranks were sent to cleanse out the temples of the capital.

19th day. Offerings were distributed to the gods of Heaven and Earth

26th day. The Ministers and public functionaries began to make votive images of Buddha for the sake of the Empress's illness.

28th day. Daibu were sent as envoys to visit the various shrines and pray for rain.

Autumn, 7th month, 7th day. At midnight, one hundred and nine habitual thieves were pardoned, and four pieces of cloth given to each. But those from the outer provinces received twenty sheaves of rice each.

12th day. Envoys were sent to pray to Hirose and Tatsuta.

29th day. The Ministers and public functionaries prepared a festival for the installation of Buddhist images in the Temple of Yakushiji.

8th month, 1st day. The Empress, having decided on this measure in the forbidden precinct, abdicated the Imperial Dignity in favor of the Prince Imperial.

END OF THE NIHONGI

Milton Keynes UK
Ingram Content Group UK Ltd.
UKHW051820300124
436936UK00004BB/312